Financial Education 101... For Students

Master Money, Build Confidence, and Secure Your Future!

Lisa Drew ED.D

Copyright © 2024 by Lisa Drew

All rights reserved. No part of this book may be reproduced, distributed, or transmitted in any form or by any means, including photocopying, recording, or other electronic or mechanical methods, without the prior written permission of the publisher, except in the case of brief quotations embodied in critical reviews and certain other noncommercial uses permitted by copyright law.

Disclaimer

This book is intended for **entertainment and educational purposes only**. The content presented here provides general information about financial concepts, strategies, and principles designed to introduce readers, particularly teens and young adults, to financial literacy. It is not a substitute for personalized financial advice and should not be considered financial, legal, or professional guidance.

Every effort has been made to ensure the information contained in this book is accurate and up-to-date at the time of publication. However, financial systems, regulations, and market conditions can change, and the information presented may not apply to all readers' specific circumstances or remain accurate over time. Readers are encouraged to consult with a qualified financial advisor, accountant, or legal professional before implementing any financial strategies or making significant financial decisions.

It is important to understand that financial literacy is a lifelong learning process, and this book serves as an introduction to foundational concepts. Individual financial situations vary widely, and what works for one person may not work for another. The examples and scenarios provided in this book are hypothetical and meant to illustrate concepts, not to guarantee specific outcomes.

By using this book, you acknowledge and agree that the author and publisher are not responsible for any actions you take based on the information provided. The advice and strategies shared are generalized and may not align with your personal financial goals or unique needs. The ultimate responsibility for your financial decisions lies with you.

For any financial actions, investments, or decisions, please seek professional advice tailored to your specific situation. This book should be seen as a supplemental resource, intended to inspire and educate readers while encouraging further exploration of financial topics.

Enjoy reading and exploring the world of financial literacy responsibly!

Permissions Requests
Requests to the publisher for permissions should be addressed to:
2227 Old Bridge Rd Woodbridge, VA. 22192 info@redcarpetbusinessexpo.com

---

Published by Lisa Drew 2227 Old Bridge Rd Woodbridge, VA. 22192
Printed in the U.S.

Table Of Contents

Chapter 1: Budgeting and Saving	7
1. How to Create a Simple Budget	9
2. The 50/30/20 Rule for Managing Money	10
3. The Importance of Tracking Expenses	11
4. How to Set Realistic Financial Goals	12
5. Why Saving a Portion of Every Paycheck Matters	13
6. The Concept of Paying Yourself First	14
7. How Compound Interest Works for Savings	15
8. The Importance of Building an Emergency Fund	16
9. Strategies to Cut Unnecessary Expenses	17
10. The Difference Between Needs and Wants	18
Chapter 2: Banking Basics	19
11. How to Open a Savings and Checking Account	21
12. How to Read and Understand a Bank Statement	22
13. The Importance of Avoiding Overdraft Fees	23
14. How to Write a Check and Balance a Checkbook	24
15. How to Use Online Banking Safely	25
16. The Benefits of Credit Unions vs. Banks	26
17. How to Protect Your Banking Information	27
18. Understanding FDIC Insurance	28
19. How to Avoid Unnecessary Banking Fees	29
20. The Importance of Regularly Monitoring Your Account	30
Chapter 3: Earning and Income	31
21. The Difference Between Gross and Net Income	35
22. How Taxes Impact Your Paycheck	36
23. The Basics of a W-4 Form	37
24. How to Read a Pay Stub	38
25. The Importance of Negotiating Salary Early in Your Career	39
26. How Side Hustles Can Supplement Income	40
27. Why Internships and Part-Time Jobs Matter	41
28. The Value of Starting a Small Business	42
29. Exploring Passive Income Opportunities	43
30. Understanding the Importance of Minimum Wage Laws	44
Chapter 3: Debt and Credit	45
31. How Credit Scores Work	48
32. What a Credit Report Is and Why It Matters	49
33. The Dangers of Credit Card Debt	50
34. The Difference Between Secured	51
and Unsecured Debt	51
35. How to Use Credit Cards Responsibly	52

36. The Importance of Paying Off Credit Card Balances in Full	53
37. How Interest Rates Affect Loans	54
38. Why Payday Loans Are a Financial Trap	55
39. How to Avoid Student Loan Debt	56
or Minimize It	56
40. The Consequences of Defaulting on a Loan	57
Chapter 4: Investing Basics	58
41. What Investing Means and Why It's Important	61
42. The Difference Between Saving and Investing	62
43. How the Stock Market Works	63
44. The Basics of Mutual Funds and ETFs	64
45. Why Starting to Invest Early Matters	65
46. The Concept of Risk vs. Reward	66
47. How to Research an Investment	67
48. The Power of Dollar-Cost Averaging	68
49. How to Diversify Your Investments	69
50. The Role of Dividends in Building Wealth	70
Chapter 5: Taxes	71
51. Why Taxes Are a Part of Life	73
52. The Basics of Income Tax Brackets	74
53. How to File a Simple Tax Return	75
54. What a W-2 Form Is and How to Use It	76
55. How Deductions and Credits Reduce Taxes	77
56. The Importance of Keeping Tax Records	78
57. The Difference Between State and Federal Taxes	79
58. How to Avoid Common Tax Scams	80
59. Understanding the Importance of Tax Refunds	81
60. Why Paying Taxes on Time Is Crucial	82
Chapter 6: Mindset and Habits	83
61. Why a Positive Money Mindset Is Essential	86
62. The Power of Delayed Gratification	87
63. How Gratitude Can Shift Your Financial Outlook	88
64. The Importance of Self-Discipline with Money	89
65. Why Failure Is Part of Financial Success	90
66. How to Set SMART Financial Goals	91
67. The Importance of Continuous Financial Education	92
68. Why Comparing Yourself to Others Can Hurt Your Finances	93
69. How Small, Consistent Steps Lead to Big Results	94
70. The Value of Celebrating Financial Milestones	95
Chapter 7: Entrepreneurship	96
71. How to Identify a Business Idea	98

72. The Basics of Creating a Business Plan	99
73. Understanding Profit and Loss	100
74. How to Market a Small Business	101
75. The Importance of Customer Service	102
76. How to Manage Business Expenses	103
77. The Basics of Registering a Business	104
78. Understanding the Role of Taxes in Business	105
79. The Value of Networking for Growth	106
80. Why Resilience Is Critical in Entrepreneurship	107
Chapter 8: Spending Wisely	108
81. How to Compare Prices Before Buying	111
82. The Importance of Reading Product Reviews	112
83. How to Avoid Impulse Purchases	113
84. Why Buying Quality Can Save Money Long-Term	114
85. How to Use Coupons and Discounts	115
86. The Value of Waiting for Sales	116
87. How to Identify and Avoid Scams	117
88. The Importance of Researching Major Purchases	118
89. The Benefits of Shopping Second-Hand	119
90. How to Calculate the True Cost of Ownership	120
Chapter9: Insurance and Protection	121
Why Should You Care Now?	123
91. The Basics of Health, Auto, Renters, and Life Insurance	127
92. Why Insurance Is a Form of Financial Protection	129
93. How Deductibles and Premiums Work	130
94. The Importance of Comparing Insurance Quotes	131
95. How to File an Insurance Claim	132
96. The Role of Life Insurance in Long-Term Planning	133
97. Why Identity Theft Protection Matters	134
98. How to Recognize Phishing Scams	135
99. The Importance of Cybersecurity for Finances	136
100. How to Create Strong Passwords for Online Accounts	137
Chapter 11- Long-Term Planning	138
101. Benefits of Lifelong Learning	144

Chapter 1: Budgeting and Saving

Learning how to budget and save is a key step toward financial freedom. Start by creating a simple budget: track your income (allowance, part-time jobs, or gifts) and expenses (like food, subscriptions, or entertainment). Categorize spending into needs (essentials) and wants (extras) to see where your money goes. If you have extra cash, save it or pay down debt. A budget isn't about restriction—it's about focusing on what matters most. As they say, *"A budget isn't a cage—it's the key to unlocking the life you truly want."*

A great way to manage money is the 50/30/20 rule: use 50% for needs, 30% for wants, and 20% for savings or debt. Even small amounts saved regularly can grow over time. Tracking expenses is also vital—use apps or a simple notebook to identify where you might be overspending. *"Tracking expenses isn't about restriction—it's about making informed choices."*

Set clear financial goals, like saving for a car or college. Be specific: "I'll save $1,000 in 10 months by putting aside $100 a month." Saving regularly, even a small portion of your income, builds financial security and opens opportunities for the future. Remember, *"Saving isn't a burden—it's a gift to your future self."*

Start building an emergency fund—even $500 can help with unexpected expenses. Cut unnecessary spending on things like unused subscriptions or frequent takeout to free up money for savings. Finally, always distinguish between needs and wants. Prioritizing essentials while allowing some room for fun is the key to balance. *"Mastering money starts with mastering choices."*

1. How to Create a Simple Budget

A budget is your financial map, guiding you toward your goals by showing you where your money is going and how much you have left to save or spend. To create one, list all your sources of income and categorize your expenses into fixed (e.g., rent, utilities) and variable (e.g., entertainment, dining out). Subtract expenses from income to see your financial standing. If there's a surplus, allocate it to savings or debt repayment. If there's a deficit, identify areas to cut back.

Mindset Shift:

Think of budgeting not as a restriction but as a tool for financial freedom. A budget isn't about saying "no" to spending but about saying "yes" to your priorities.

Tips:

- Use a budgeting app like Mint, YNAB, or PocketGuard for easier tracking.
- Include a category for fun money to prevent burnout from excessive restrictions.
- Review your budget every month and adjust it based on changes in income or expenses.

Quote:

"A budget isn't a cage—it's the key to unlocking the life you truly want."

2. The 50/30/20 Rule for Managing Money

The 50/30/20 rule provides a simple framework for managing your money effectively. It allocates 50% of your income to needs (housing, groceries, bills), 30% to wants (entertainment, hobbies), and 20% to savings or debt repayment. This balance ensures you're covering necessities while still enjoying life and building financial security.

Mindset Shift:
Money isn't just for surviving; it's for thriving. A structured approach like the 50/30/20 rule ensures you're not only meeting today's needs but also preparing for tomorrow's dreams.

Tips:
- Track your spending for a month to see if your current allocations align with the rule.
- Adjust the percentages if your financial goals or living situation demand it (e.g., saving 30% instead of 20%).
- Automate savings to ensure the 20% is prioritized.

Quote:
"Balance is the art of living fully today while safeguarding your future."

3. The Importance of Tracking Expenses

Tracking expenses gives you a clear picture of where your money is going. It reveals spending patterns, identifies unnecessary expenses, and ensures you stay within your budget. Without tracking, it's easy to lose control of your finances and wonder why there's "never enough money."

Mindset Shift:
Think of expense tracking as self-awareness for your finances. Just as you can't improve your health without knowing your diet, you can't improve your finances without knowing your spending.

Tips:

- Use tools like spreadsheets or apps (e.g., Spendee, Personal Capital) for ease and accuracy.
- Categorize every expense to see where you can cut back (e.g., dining out, subscriptions).
- Set a reminder to review your expenses weekly.

Quote:
"Tracking expenses isn't about restriction—it's about empowerment to make informed choices."

4. How to Set Realistic Financial Goals

Setting financial goals gives your money purpose. Goals should follow the **SMART** framework: Specific, Measurable, Achievable, Relevant, and Time-bound. For example, instead of saying, "I want to save money," aim for, "I'll save $5,000 for an emergency fund in 12 months by saving $420 each month."

Mindset Shift:
Goals turn abstract desires into actionable plans. Each goal is a step toward the life you envision, so make them as concrete and inspiring as possible.

Tips:

- Write down your goals and place them somewhere visible.
- Break big goals into smaller milestones to stay motivated.
- Celebrate small wins to build momentum toward larger achievements.

Quote:
"Dreams become reality when you give them deadlines and take consistent action."

5. Why Saving a Portion of Every Paycheck Matters

Saving regularly builds a financial cushion, reduces stress, and supports long-term goals. Even saving a small portion, like 10% of your paycheck, creates momentum. Over time, these contributions grow into substantial savings, thanks to consistency and compound interest.

Mindset Shift:
Think of saving not as sacrificing today's pleasures but as investing in tomorrow's opportunities. Every dollar saved is a step closer to financial freedom.

Tips:
- Automate savings to ensure consistency and avoid the temptation to skip.
- Start small if needed, and gradually increase your savings rate.
- Open a separate high-yield savings account to grow your money faster.

Quote:
"Saving isn't a burden—it's a gift to your future self."

6. The Concept of Paying Yourself First

Paying yourself first means setting aside money for savings and investments before paying bills or spending on discretionary items. This habit ensures your financial goals are prioritized over impulsive spending. By automating this process, you remove the temptation to spend what should be saved.

Mindset Shift:
You work hard for your money—make sure you're using it to secure your future before funding someone else's priorities (like retailers or service providers).

Tips:

- Set up automatic transfers to savings accounts or investment platforms on payday.
- Allocate at least 10-20% of your income toward paying yourself first.
- Reward yourself occasionally to stay motivated and consistent.

Quote:
"Paying yourself first is the ultimate act of self-respect—because your dreams deserve to come first."

7. How Compound Interest Works for Savings

Compound interest allows your money to grow exponentially over time. Unlike simple interest, which is calculated only on the principal, compound interest earns interest on both the principal and previously earned interest. Starting early is key to maximizing its power.

Mindset Shift:
Time is your greatest ally when it comes to growing wealth. The sooner you start saving, the less you'll need to save later to achieve the same goal.

Tips:

- Start saving or investing as early as possible, even in small amounts.
- Choose accounts with higher interest rates, like high-yield savings accounts or index funds.
- Let your money grow by reinvesting interest or dividends.

Quote:
"Compound interest is the snowball effect of money—small steps today lead to monumental growth tomorrow."

8. The Importance of Building an Emergency Fund

An emergency fund is a financial buffer for unexpected expenses like car repairs, medical bills, or job loss. Aim to save 3-6 months' worth of living expenses to avoid debt in crises. This fund ensures stability and peace of mind when life throws curveballs.

Mindset Shift:
Think of an emergency fund as a shield, not a luxury. It's about protecting your future from life's uncertainties, not just saving for a rainy day.

Tips:

- Start small—$500 is a great initial goal.
- Keep the fund in a separate account to avoid the temptation to dip into it.
- Replenish the fund immediately after using it.

Quote:
"An emergency fund is more than money—it's peace of mind and freedom from financial stress."

9. Strategies to Cut Unnecessary Expenses

Reducing unnecessary expenses frees up money for savings, investments, or debt repayment. Common areas to cut include dining out, unused subscriptions, and impulse purchases. Evaluate your spending habits to identify where you can trim costs without sacrificing quality of life.

Mindset Shift:
Cutting expenses isn't about deprivation—it's about aligning your spending with your values and goals. Every dollar saved is a step toward freedom.

Tips:

- Audit your subscriptions and cancel the ones you rarely use.
- Meal prep to save on dining costs.
- Implement a 24-hour rule for purchases to avoid impulse spending.

Quote:
"Spend intentionally—save where you can so you can splurge where it truly matters."

10. The Difference Between Needs and Wants

Needs are essentials required for living, such as housing, food, and utilities. Wants are non-essential items that enhance life, like designer clothes or a streaming subscription. Prioritizing needs ensures your basic financial stability before allocating funds to wants.

Mindset Shift:
Distinguishing needs from wants isn't about denial—it's about ensuring your foundation is secure before building on it.

Tips:

- Before purchasing, ask yourself: "Do I need this, or do I just want it?"
- Limit wants to a specific percentage of your budget (e.g., 20%).
- Periodically review spending habits to ensure alignment with goals.

Quote:
"Mastering your money starts with mastering your choices—needs to sustain you, and enhance you."

Chapter 2: Banking Basics

Understanding banking basics is essential for managing your money effectively. The two most common types of accounts are checking and savings accounts. Checking accounts are designed for everyday transactions like paying bills or using a debit card, while savings accounts help you store money you don't need immediately and earn interest over time. Opening an account is simple—just bring a valid ID, your Social Security Number, and a small deposit (if required). You can open accounts in person, online, or through a mobile app.

Banks offer tools like debit and credit cards to help manage spending. A debit card is linked to your checking account, while a credit card allows you to borrow money and pay it back later, helping you build credit if used responsibly. Online banking and mobile apps make it easy to check balances, transfer money, and pay bills. Direct deposit lets your paycheck go straight into your account, and ATMs provide convenient cash access.

It's also important to understand bank fees, such as maintenance fees, ATM fees, and overdraft charges. Choosing a bank with low or no fees and monitoring your account regularly can help you avoid unnecessary costs. Saving money is another critical part of banking. A savings account can grow your money through interest, helping you achieve both short-term and long-term goals. Look for accounts with competitive interest rates and no fees to maximize your savings.

Finally, prioritize security by safeguarding your account information, using strong passwords, and enabling two-factor authentication. Most banks in the U.S. protect your deposits with FDIC insurance, which covers up to $250,000 per account. Banking is a powerful tool to manage your money and build financial security—start with the basics, and take advantage of the resources your bank offers to achieve your goals.

11. How to Open a Savings and Checking Account

A checking account is designed for everyday transactions, while a savings account helps you set aside money for future needs. Opening these accounts involves choosing a financial institution, gathering the required documents (government-issued ID, Social Security Number, and proof of address), and making an initial deposit. Banks and credit unions often provide options to open accounts in person or online. It's essential to compare account features like minimum balance requirements, fees, and interest rates.

Tips:

1. Research Account Options: Look for accounts with low fees, no minimum balance requirements, and perks like interest on savings or cashback.
2. Prepare Documents: Bring valid identification, proof of address (e.g., utility bill), and your Social Security Number.
3. Start Small: Open both a checking and savings account simultaneously to establish good financial habits.
4. Ask About Fees: Ensure you understand monthly maintenance fees and how to avoid them.
5. Opt for Online Access: Choose an account with robust online or mobile banking features for easy management.

Mindset Shift:
Think of your bank accounts as tools to help you organize and grow your money. They're the foundation of your financial health.

Quote:
"A bank account is more than a place to hold money—it's the launchpad for your financial goals."

12. How to Read and Understand a Bank Statement

A bank statement is a record of all account activity within a specific period, usually monthly. It includes deposits, withdrawals, fees, and the opening and closing balances. Understanding your statement is crucial for identifying unauthorized transactions, tracking expenses, and ensuring accuracy in your account.

Tips:

1. Review Regularly: Make it a habit to read your statement monthly to spot discrepancies or fraudulent activity.
2. Check for Errors: Look for incorrect charges or unrecognized transactions and report them immediately.
3. Track Recurring Payments: Verify subscriptions, memberships, or automatic bill payments.
4. Understand Key Terms: Familiarize yourself with terms like "debit," "credit," "cleared," and "pending."
5. Use Statements for Budgeting: Analyze spending categories to adjust your budget effectively.

Mindset Shift:
Think of your bank statement as a report card for your finances. Understanding it helps you make informed decisions about your money.

Quote:
"Your bank statement tells the story of your financial habits—read it carefully to shape the next chapter."

13. The Importance of Avoiding Overdraft Fees

Overdraft fees occur when you spend more than your account balance, and the bank covers the difference. These fees can range from $30 to $50 per transaction and add up quickly if not managed. Avoiding overdraft fees requires careful monitoring of your account and understanding the terms of your overdraft protection.

Tips:

1. Set Up Alerts: Use banking alerts to notify you when your balance drops below a certain threshold.
2. Opt Out of Overdraft Protection: This prevents your account from being charged when you don't have sufficient funds.
3. Maintain a Buffer: Keep a minimum balance in your account as a safety net.
4. Link Accounts: Link your checking account to your savings account for overdraft protection.
5. Track Transactions: Record every withdrawal and payment to avoid overdrafts.

Mindset Shift:
Overdraft fees are preventable expenses. By staying vigilant, you save money and maintain financial control.

Quote:
"Overdraft fees are the cost of inattention—stay alert to keep your money where it belongs."

14. How to Write a Check and Balance a Checkbook

Writing a check involves filling out fields like the date, payee, amount, and memo line, then signing it. Balancing a checkbook means keeping a record of all transactions (checks, ATM withdrawals, deposits) and reconciling them with your bank statement to ensure accuracy.

Tips:

1. Practice Writing Checks: Use legible handwriting and double-check details before issuing.
2. Keep a Check Register: Record every check, withdrawal, and deposit to track your account.
3. Reconcile Monthly: Compare your checkbook with your bank statement to spot errors or missed entries.
4. Avoid Post-Dating Checks: Ensure funds are available when writing a check.
5. Use Online Resources: Leverage apps or spreadsheets for modern checkbook balancing.

Mindset Shift:
Balancing your checkbook may feel outdated but remains a critical skill for financial accountability.

Quote:
"Every dollar counts—balancing your checkbook ensures no penny goes unaccounted for."

15. How to Use Online Banking Safely

Online banking simplifies account management, but it also requires vigilance to protect against fraud. Accessing your account through secure platforms allows you to pay bills, transfer funds, and monitor balances from anywhere.

Tips:

1. Use Strong Passwords: Combine uppercase letters, lowercase letters, numbers, and special characters.
2. Enable Two-Factor Authentication: Add an extra layer of security to your account login.
3. Avoid Public Wi-Fi: Use secure networks or a VPN when accessing your account.
4. Log Out After Use: Especially on shared devices.
5. Monitor Regularly: Check your account for unauthorized transactions.

Mindset Shift:
Convenience doesn't mean complacency. Safe online banking protects both your time and your money.

Quote:
"Digital access demands digital vigilance—secure your account to secure your peace of mind."

16. The Benefits of Credit Unions vs. Banks

Credit unions are member-owned, not-for-profit institutions offering lower fees and higher interest rates on savings, while banks provide a broader range of services and a more extensive branch network. Choosing between the two depends on your financial needs and priorities.

Tips:
1. Compare Fees: Credit unions often waive monthly fees or require lower minimum balances.
2. Consider Interest Rates: Credit unions typically offer better rates on savings and loans.
3. Weigh Accessibility: Banks usually have more branches and ATMs.
4. Look for Personalized Service: Credit unions often provide a more community-oriented experience.
5. Evaluate Technology: Banks usually have more advanced digital tools.

Mindset Shift:
The best financial institution isn't about size—it's about how well it fits your financial goals.

Quote:
"Choosing a financial partner is about trust—credit unions offer community, while banks provide convenience."

17. How to Protect Your Banking Information

Fraud and identity theft are risks in today's digital world. Protecting your banking information involves safeguarding account numbers, passwords, and sensitive documents.

Tips:

1. Monitor Accounts Daily: Spot unauthorized transactions early.
2. Use Secure Passwords: Avoid reusing passwords across platforms.
3. Shred Financial Documents: Prevent thieves from accessing personal information.
4. Beware of Phishing Scams: Don't click on suspicious links or share details over email.
5. Enable Notifications: Set up transaction alerts for instant updates.

Mindset Shift:
Your financial information is as valuable as the money in your account—guard it fiercely.

Quote:
"Security starts with awareness—protecting your banking information protects your financial future."

18. Understanding FDIC Insurance

The Federal Deposit Insurance Corporation (FDIC) insures deposits at participating banks up to $250,000 per depositor, per account type. This guarantees your money is safe even if the bank fails.

Tips:

1. Verify FDIC Coverage: Ensure your bank is FDIC-insured before opening an account.
2. Understand Coverage Limits: Spread funds across multiple banks if necessary.
3. Know What's Covered: FDIC insurance applies to checking, savings, and CDs but not investments.

Mindset Shift:
FDIC insurance provides peace of mind. Knowing your money is protected allows you to focus on financial growth.

Quote:
"FDIC insurance is your safety net—because peace of mind is priceless."

19. How to Avoid Unnecessary Banking Fees

Banking fees can chip away at your savings over time. These include maintenance fees, ATM surcharges, and overdraft charges. Being aware of these costs helps you save money.

Tips:

1. Choose Fee-Free Accounts: Many banks and credit unions offer no-fee options.
2. Stay In-Network: Use your bank's ATMs to avoid surcharges.
3. Maintain Minimum Balances: Avoid penalties by meeting account requirements.
4. Ask for Waivers: Some banks waive fees for students or direct deposit users.
5. Review Terms Regularly: Be aware of changes in account fees or conditions.

Mindset Shift:
Banking fees are avoidable. Every dollar saved is a dollar earned toward your financial goals.

Quote:
"Bank smarter, not harder—every fee avoided is a step closer to financial freedom."

20. The Importance of Regularly Monitoring Your Account

Regular account monitoring ensures you're aware of your financial health. It helps you catch unauthorized transactions, manage spending, and avoid overdrafts.

Tips:

1. Set Alerts: Receive notifications for large transactions or low balances.
2. Review Weekly: Make it a habit to check your account every few days.
3. Track Spending Trends: Use online tools to categorize and analyze your expenses.
4. Spot Fraud Early: Report suspicious activity immediately to minimize losses.
5. Reconcile Transactions: Match your account activity with receipts for accuracy.

Mindset Shift:
Monitoring your account isn't about paranoia—it's about financial awareness and control.

Quote:
"Master your money by staying informed—regular account checks are the key to financial empowerment."

Chapter 3: Earning and Income

Earning income is one of the most empowering steps toward achieving financial independence and building the life you envision. It's more than just covering bills or saving for the next big purchase—it's about creating opportunities, opening doors, and setting yourself up for long-term success. Your journey to financial freedom starts with recognizing the value of every dollar you earn and taking intentional steps to maximize your potential.

Income comes in many forms, and understanding these is key to making the most of your earning power. **Earned income**, such as wages, salaries, or tips, is the most common starting point. Whether it's a part-time job, freelancing gig, or entrepreneurial venture, every opportunity helps you develop skills and build confidence.

Don't underestimate the power of starting small—every step forward is progress. At the same time, explore avenues for **passive income**, such as renting out property, selling digital products, or earning royalties from creative work. This type of income works for you even when you're not actively working. **Portfolio income**, generated through investments like dividends or stock gains, allows your money to grow and multiply over time, giving you another way to build wealth.

Finding opportunities to earn is easier than you might think if you stay open-minded and creative. Start with what you know—whether it's a talent, skill, or hobby—and find ways to monetize it. Platforms like Etsy, Fiverr, and social media make it easier than ever to connect with people who need your services or products. If you're just starting out, part-time jobs or internships not only provide income but also give you real-world experience that boosts your confidence and résumé. Remember, the journey isn't just about making money—it's about learning and growing along the way.

As you gain experience, focus on increasing your earning potential. Invest in yourself by pursuing education, certifications, or skill-building opportunities. Every new skill you acquire becomes a tool in your arsenal, opening doors to higher-paying roles and more fulfilling work. Build your network, because relationships often lead to opportunities that hard work alone might not uncover. Surround yourself with people who inspire and challenge you to grow. The effort you put into personal development today will pay off exponentially in the future.

Once you start earning, managing your income effectively is critical to turning your hard work into lasting financial security. Budgeting may not sound glamorous, but it's a powerful tool that ensures your money works for you. Start by tracking your income and expenses, allocating funds to necessities, wants, and savings. Saving regularly, even if it's just a small amount, builds momentum and creates a sense of accomplishment. Don't fall into the trap of lifestyle inflation—earning more doesn't mean spending more. Instead, focus on putting your money to work by investing in your future.

Passive income streams are where financial freedom becomes a reality. Imagine earning money while you sleep—whether it's through dividends, rental properties, or a successful online course. While these opportunities may take time and effort to build, they are worth the investment. Passive income allows you to focus less on the grind and more on what truly matters to you, whether that's family, hobbies, or pursuing your dreams.

Your journey to earning income is about more than just financial gain—it's about creating the life you want, step by step. Don't be afraid to dream big and start small. Every dollar earned is a brick in the foundation of your future. Stay motivated, stay disciplined, and remember: the effort you put in today is an investment in the life you'll enjoy tomorrow. You have the power to build something incredible—start now, and keep moving forward.

21. The Difference Between Gross and Net Income

Gross income is your total earnings before any deductions, including taxes, retirement contributions, and insurance premiums. Net income, often referred to as "take-home pay," is what's left after these deductions are subtracted. Understanding the difference helps you budget effectively and set realistic financial goals.

Tips:

1. Review your pay stub to see the breakdown between gross and net income.
2. Use gross income for long-term financial planning and net income for day-to-day budgeting.
3. Factor in deductions when evaluating job offers or planning major expenses.

Mindset Shift:
Think of gross income as the potential and net income as the reality. Budgeting starts with knowing what you truly bring home.

Quote:
"Gross income shows your worth; net income shows your reality—master both to build your financial future."

22. How Taxes Impact Your Paycheck

Taxes significantly reduce your gross income to determine your net pay. Common deductions include federal and state income taxes, Social Security, and Medicare. Understanding these deductions helps you anticipate your actual earnings and avoid surprises.

Tips:

1. Learn your tax bracket to estimate how much will be withheld.
2. Use a paycheck calculator to understand how deductions impact your pay.
3. Review your W-4 form regularly to adjust withholdings for life changes (e.g., marriage, dependents).

Mindset Shift:
Taxes are a part of life, but understanding them empowers you to plan and manage your finances effectively.

Quote:
"Taxes may be inevitable, but surprise tax deductions aren't—know where your money goes to take control of your paycheck."

23. The Basics of a W-4 Form

The W-4 form tells your employer how much federal income tax to withhold from your paycheck. Filling it out correctly ensures you don't owe a large sum or get an unnecessarily large refund come tax time.

Tips:
1. Update your W-4 whenever you experience a major life event (marriage, new child, etc.).
2. Use the IRS's online tax withholding estimator to determine the right allowances.
3. Check your withholding annually to avoid over- or under-paying taxes.

Mindset Shift:
Your W-4 is a tool for financial precision. Take the time to understand it, and you'll keep more control over your money.

Quote:
"Filling out a W-4 isn't just paperwork—it's a step toward smarter financial planning."

24. How to Read a Pay Stub

A pay stub is a breakdown of your earnings, deductions, and net pay for a specific pay period. It includes sections for gross income, federal and state tax withholdings, Social Security, Medicare, and other deductions like health insurance.

Tips:

1. Pay attention to gross income, net income, and deductions.
2. Look for additional contributions, like 401(k) deposits, to ensure accuracy.
3. Check for errors in hours worked or overtime pay.

Mindset Shift:
Think of your pay stub as a financial mirror. Understanding its details reflects your control over your earnings.

Quote:
"A pay stub isn't just a piece of paper—it's your financial reality, laid bare."

25. The Importance of Negotiating Salary Early in Your Career

Negotiating your starting salary has a compounding effect on your lifetime earnings. Even a small increase early on can result in significantly higher income over time due to raises and bonuses tied to your base salary.

Tips:

1. Research industry standards for your position to set realistic expectations.
2. Highlight your skills and achievements to justify a higher offer.
3. Practice negotiation techniques to build confidence.

Mindset Shift:
Negotiation isn't about greed—it's about valuing your worth and setting a strong financial foundation.

Quote:
"Your first salary sets the tone for your financial journey—ask for what you're worth, because you're worth it."

26. How Side Hustles Can Supplement Income

A side hustle is an additional job or freelance work that generates extra income. It can help you pay off debt, build savings, or fund hobbies without relying solely on your main job.

Tips:

1. Choose a side hustle that aligns with your skills or passions.
2. Set clear goals for what the extra income will achieve (e.g., savings, vacation).
3. Manage your time effectively to avoid burnout.

Mindset Shift:
A side hustle isn't just extra work—it's an opportunity to accelerate your financial goals.

Quote:
"Side hustles turn spare hours into extra dollars—fueling your dreams one gig at a time."

27. Why Internships and Part-Time Jobs Matter

Internships and part-time jobs provide valuable experience, build professional networks, and help you develop skills. They also introduce you to workplace dynamics, preparing you for full-time roles.

Tips:

1. Choose opportunities that align with your career goals or interests.
2. Treat every role as a learning experience, no matter how small the task.
3. Network with colleagues to build connections that can open future doors.

Mindset Shift:
An internship or part-time job isn't just about money—it's an investment in your future career and financial success.

Quote:
"Experience is the currency of opportunity—internships and part-time jobs are your first deposit."

28. The Value of Starting a Small Business

A small business provides autonomy and the potential for unlimited earnings. It teaches you how to manage finances, market products or services, and build a brand. While challenging, entrepreneurship can be deeply rewarding.

Tips:

1. Start small to minimize risks—test your idea before scaling.
2. Create a solid business plan to guide your strategy.
3. Use social media and word-of-mouth marketing to build your customer base.

Mindset Shift:
A small business isn't just a source of income—it's a pathway to independence and personal growth.

Quote:
"Every big success starts small—your small business is the seed of financial freedom."

29. Exploring Passive Income Opportunities

Passive income is money earned with minimal ongoing effort, such as rental income, investments, or royalties. It diversifies your income streams and provides financial stability.

Tips:

1. Start with small, manageable investments (e.g., index funds, REITs).
2. Explore skills-based passive income, like selling digital products or writing a book.
3. Reinvest earnings to grow your passive income over time.

Mindset Shift:
Passive income isn't about doing nothing—it's about working smarter to make your money work for you.

Quote:
"Passive income is freedom in action—it works while you rest, building your wealth around the clock."

30. Understanding the Importance of Minimum Wage Laws

Minimum wage laws ensure workers receive fair compensation for their labor. These laws protect vulnerable workers and establish a baseline for income, helping reduce poverty and improve living standards.

Tips:

1. Research your local minimum wage to understand your rights.
2. Advocate for fair pay if you believe your wages don't reflect your value.
3. Use minimum wage jobs as stepping stones, building skills and experience for higher-paying roles.

Mindset Shift:
Minimum wage isn't the ceiling—it's the foundation for growth. Use it as a starting point, not a stopping point.

Quote:
"Minimum wage is the floor of opportunity—step up from it to build a better future."

Chapter 3: Debt and Credit

Debt and credit are essential components of personal finance, offering opportunities to achieve goals like buying a home, funding education, or starting a business. However, they require careful management to avoid pitfalls that can hinder financial stability. Credit allows you to borrow money with the promise to repay it later, often with interest. It comes in many forms, such as credit cards, personal loans, car loans, and mortgages.

Your ability to access credit depends on your **credit score**, a numerical representation of your financial trustworthiness. This score is influenced by several factors, including your payment history, the amount of credit you use relative to your limit (credit utilization), the length of your credit history, and the types of credit you have. A strong credit score can unlock lower interest rates, higher borrowing limits, and better financial opportunities.

When it comes to debt, not all types are created equal. **Good debt** is an investment in your future, such as a mortgage for a home, student loans for education, or a business loan to fund a venture. These types of debt can lead to increased income or long-term financial growth, making them strategic choices when used wisely. On the other hand, **bad debt** often involves borrowing for depreciating assets or unnecessary purchases, such as credit card debt for luxury items or payday loans with excessively high interest rates. The distinction between good and bad debt lies in whether the debt serves a meaningful purpose and fits within your financial plan.

Using credit wisely is key to maintaining financial health. Always pay bills on time to avoid late fees and protect your credit score, as payment history is the most significant factor affecting it. Keep your credit card balances low, ideally under 30% of your credit limit, to maintain a healthy credit utilization ratio. Building credit early can also set you up for future financial success; for example, opening a secured or student credit card and using it responsibly can help establish a strong credit history. Regularly checking your credit report is another essential habit. Reviewing your report for errors or signs of identity theft ensures your financial record remains accurate and secure.

Managing debt effectively is another critical aspect of financial well-being. Start by understanding the total amount you owe and the terms of each loan, including interest rates and repayment schedules. Two popular strategies for tackling multiple debts are the **debt snowball method** and the **debt avalanche method**. The debt snowball method focuses on paying off the smallest debts first, giving you quick wins and building momentum as you tackle larger balances. In contrast, the debt avalanche method prioritizes debts with the highest interest rates, helping you save more money over time. Choose the approach that best fits your financial situation and motivates you to stay on track.

While debt and credit can be intimidating, they are also powerful tools when used responsibly. They provide the means to achieve significant milestones and build a strong financial foundation. By understanding how to use credit wisely, distinguish between good and bad debt, and manage obligations effectively, you can leverage these tools to create financial stability and set yourself up for long-term success. Remember, the key to mastering debt and credit lies in intentionality—borrowing for meaningful purposes, staying disciplined with repayments, and planning for the future. With a thoughtful approach, you can turn debt and credit into stepping stones toward achieving your financial dreams.

31. How Credit Scores Work

A credit score is a three-digit number, typically ranging from 300 to 850, that reflects your creditworthiness. It's calculated based on factors like payment history, credit utilization, length of credit history, credit mix, and new credit inquiries. Lenders use it to assess your ability to repay loans or credit.

Why It Matters:

- A higher credit score qualifies you for lower interest rates.
- A poor score can limit access to loans, apartments, or even jobs.

Tips:

1. Pay all bills on time to maintain a positive payment history (35% of your score).
2. Keep your credit utilization under 30% of your total credit limit.
3. Check your score regularly for accuracy.

Mindset Shift:
Your credit score isn't about how much you earn—it's about how responsibly you manage credit.

Quote:
"A good credit score is a key to financial opportunities—build it consistently to unlock your future."

32. What a Credit Report Is and Why It Matters

A credit report is a detailed summary of your credit history, maintained by credit bureaus (Experian, Equifax, TransUnion). It includes account balances, payment history, credit limits, inquiries, and any derogatory marks like late payments or defaults.

Why It Matters:

- Lenders and landlords check it to assess your financial reliability.
- Errors can harm your credit score, affecting loan approval.

Tips:

1. Obtain your free credit report yearly at AnnualCreditReport.com.
2. Dispute inaccuracies immediately with the credit bureau.
3. Use the report to identify areas for improvement.

Mindset Shift:
Your credit report is your financial résumé—keeping it clean ensures you're always ready for opportunities.

Quote:
"Your credit report reflects your financial habits—ensure it tells the right story."

33. The Dangers of Credit Card Debt

Credit card debt accumulates quickly due to high-interest rates, often over 20%. It limits your ability to save and invest while damaging your credit score if balances remain unpaid.

Why It Matters:

- Interest compounds, making debt harder to eliminate.
- High utilization negatively affects your credit score.

Tips:

1. Avoid spending more than you can pay off each month.
2. Focus on paying down high-interest cards first.
3. Limit credit card use to essential, planned purchases.

Mindset Shift:
Credit cards are tools, not lifelines. Use them wisely to build credit, not accumulate debt.

Quote:
"Credit card debt grows faster than you think—don't let today's convenience sabotage tomorrow's financial health."

34. The Difference Between Secured and Unsecured Debt

Secured debt is backed by collateral, such as a car or house, which the lender can repossess if you fail to repay. Unsecured debt, like credit card balances or personal loans, doesn't require collateral but usually carries higher interest rates.

Why It Matters:

- Secured loans often offer lower interest rates but come with the risk of losing your collateral.
- Unsecured loans rely on your creditworthiness.

Tips:

1. Use secured loans for large, necessary purchases (e.g., homes or cars).
2. Avoid high-interest unsecured loans for discretionary spending.
3. Always understand the terms before borrowing.

Mindset Shift:
Debt is a tool—secured or unsecured, it's how you use it that determines its impact.

Quote:
"Debt can build or break your financial stability—know its cost before you commit."

35. How to Use Credit Cards Responsibly

Credit cards can build your credit score and offer convenience, but only if used responsibly. Treat your credit card like cash and avoid spending more than you can pay off monthly.

Why It Matters:

- Responsible credit card use builds a positive credit history.
- Mismanagement can lead to debt and a damaged credit score.

Tips:

1. Pay balances in full every month to avoid interest.
2. Use cards for budgeted expenses only (e.g., groceries, gas).
3. Monitor your spending and set alerts for payment due dates.

Mindset Shift:
A credit card isn't a ticket to spend more—it's a tool to grow your credit while staying within your means.

Quote:
"Responsible credit card use turns debt into an opportunity, not a burden."

36. The Importance of Paying Off Credit Card Balances in Full

Paying your credit card balance in full every month avoids interest charges and improves your credit score by keeping your utilization low.

Why It Matters:

- Interest compounds, increasing the cost of unpaid balances.
- Full payments prevent debt accumulation and improve your creditworthiness.

Tips:

1. Budget credit card payments as a fixed monthly expense.
2. Set up automatic payments to ensure you never miss a due date.
3. Avoid carrying balances, even small ones, as interest adds up quickly.

Mindset Shift:
Carrying a balance is not financial progress—it's a preventable expense that drains your resources.

Quote:
"Paying off your balance in full is an act of financial discipline—it saves you money and builds your future."

---

37. How Interest Rates Affect Loans

Interest rates determine how much you pay to borrow money. Higher rates increase your total repayment, while lower rates make borrowing more affordable.

Why It Matters:

- A lower interest rate saves money over the life of a loan.
- High rates can make loans unaffordable, leading to missed payments.

Tips:

1. Compare lenders to find the lowest interest rates.
2. Improve your credit score to qualify for better rates.
3. Pay more than the minimum payment to reduce interest over time.

Mindset Shift:
Interest is the price of borrowing—minimizing it maximizes your financial potential.

Quote:
"Every percentage point saved on interest is a step closer to financial freedom."

38. Why Payday Loans Are a Financial Trap

Payday loans are short-term loans with extremely high interest rates, often exceeding 400%. They create a cycle of debt that's hard to escape, especially if you roll over the loan into new terms.

Why It Matters:

- High fees and interest rates can multiply the original loan amount.
- Defaulting on payday loans can damage your credit and financial stability.

Tips:

1. Avoid payday loans—explore alternatives like personal loans, credit unions, or borrowing from friends.
2. Build an emergency fund to handle unexpected expenses.
3. Seek financial counseling if you're struggling with debt.

Mindset Shift:
Payday loans offer quick fixes but lead to long-term financial traps—preparation is the best solution.

Quote:
"Payday loans promise relief but deliver regret—choose smarter alternatives for lasting solutions."

39. How to Avoid Student Loan Debt or Minimize It

Student loans can burden you for decades, but strategic planning can minimize or avoid debt entirely.

Why It Matters:

- Excessive debt limits your financial flexibility after graduation.
- Scholarships and grants can reduce the need for loans.

Tips:

1. Apply for as many scholarships and grants as possible.
2. Attend community college or in-state universities to save on tuition.
3. Borrow only what you need—don't accept the full loan offer if it exceeds your expenses.

Mindset Shift:
Student loans are an investment, not free money—borrow wisely to avoid regrets.

Quote:
"Education opens doors, but smart borrowing ensures those doors remain unlocked."

40. The Consequences of Defaulting on a Loan

Defaulting on a loan occurs when you fail to meet repayment terms, leading to severe consequences like damaged credit, legal action, and difficulty obtaining future loans.

Why It Matters:

- Defaults remain on your credit report for up to seven years.
- Secured loans may result in the loss of collateral (e.g., your home or car).

Tips:

1. Communicate with your lender early if you're struggling—they may offer deferment or forbearance.
2. Prioritize loan payments in your budget to avoid defaulting.
3. Consider refinancing or consolidating loans for lower monthly payments.

Mindset Shift:
Defaulting isn't the end, but it's a setback—proactive planning prevents long-term damage.

Quote:
"Defaulting on a loan damages more than your credit—it derails your financial future. Plan to stay ahead."

Chapter 4: Investing Basics

Investing is one of the smartest ways to grow your money and prepare for big goals, whether it's saving for college, buying a car, starting a business, or building long-term wealth. The earlier you start investing, the more time your money has to grow, thanks to the power of *compound interest*. This is when your investments earn returns, and those returns start earning their own returns, creating exponential growth. For young people, investing can seem intimidating or like something you'll "figure out later," but starting now—even with a small amount—can make a huge difference in your future.

To make investing simple and approachable, think of the acronym **G.R.O.W.**:

- **G:** *Goals* – Start by identifying why you want to invest. Are you saving for something specific, like a new laptop or a down payment on a house? Or are you thinking about your long-term future, like retirement? Setting clear goals helps you stay focused and choose the right investments.
- **R:** *Risk* – Understand your risk tolerance. Stocks, for example, have the potential for high growth but can be unpredictable in the short term. Bonds are safer but

typically offer smaller returns. As a young investor, you can often afford to take more risks because you have time to recover from any losses. The key is to balance risk and reward in a way that feels comfortable for you.

- O: *Options* – Learn about the different types of investments available. **Stocks** give you a small ownership stake in a company and can grow significantly over time. **Bonds** are loans to companies or governments and provide steady, predictable returns. **Index funds** or **ETFs** (Exchange-Traded Funds) are collections of stocks or bonds that give you instant diversification, making them a great choice for beginners. Diversification reduces risk because your money is spread across many different assets rather than relying on just one.
- W: *Watch* – While it's important to keep an eye on your investments, avoid the temptation to check them constantly or panic when markets dip. Investing is a long-term game, and the market naturally goes up and down. Staying patient and focused on your goals will help you succeed over time.

Getting started with investing doesn't require a lot of money. Many platforms allow you to open an account with as little as $10 or $20. Begin by opening a brokerage account, retirement account like a Roth IRA, or a robo-advisor, which can automatically manage your investments based on your goals and risk tolerance. Start small by contributing to low-cost **index funds** or **ETFs**, which offer a diversified and affordable way to invest. Even setting aside $20 or $50 each month can add up significantly over time.

One of the most powerful things about investing as a young person is that time is on your side. For example, if you invest $50 a month starting at age 18, earning an average return of 7%, you could have over $120,000 by age 50. If you wait until you're 30 to start, you'd only have about $40,000 with the same contributions. This difference is because of *compound interest*, which allows your money to grow exponentially the earlier you start.

Investing isn't just for older adults or wealthy people—it's for anyone who wants to take control of their financial future. By starting now, even with small steps, you're setting yourself up for long-term success. With the **G.R.O.W.** mindset, you can begin building wealth today, creating opportunities and financial security for tomorrow. Take the leap, invest in your future, and watch your money grow. The sooner you start, the more powerful the results will be!

41. What Investing Means and Why It's Important

Investing is the act of putting your money into assets like stocks, bonds, real estate, or businesses with the expectation of generating a return over time. It's an essential tool for building wealth, achieving financial goals, and outpacing inflation.

Why It Matters:

- Investments grow your money faster than traditional savings accounts.
- They help you achieve long-term goals like retirement or buying a home.
- Investing builds financial independence.

Tips:

1. Start small and gradually increase your investment contributions.
2. Focus on long-term growth rather than short-term gains.
3. Learn the basics of different asset types to diversify your portfolio.

Mindset Shift:
Investing is about planting seeds today for a better tomorrow. The earlier you start, the bigger the harvest.

Quote:
"Investing turns your money into a worker—put it to work for your dreams."

42. The Difference Between Saving and Investing

Saving involves setting aside money in safe, easily accessible accounts for short-term goals or emergencies. Investing, on the other hand, means putting money into assets that can grow over time but come with varying levels of risk.

Why It Matters:

- Savings provide security for immediate needs, while investments build long-term wealth.
- Both are essential for financial health.

Tips:

1. Save 3-6 months of living expenses in an emergency fund before investing.
2. Use high-yield savings accounts for short-term goals.
3. Invest for long-term goals like retirement or wealth building.

Mindset Shift:
Saving keeps you safe; investing helps you grow. Both are tools for different stages of your financial journey.

Quote:
"Savings protect your today; investments secure your tomorrow."

43. How the Stock Market Works

The stock market is a marketplace where investors buy and sell shares of companies. Companies issue shares to raise money, and investors purchase them to gain ownership stakes. Share prices fluctuate based on supply, demand, and market sentiment.

Why It Matters:

- The stock market offers opportunities for wealth growth through capital appreciation and dividends.
- Understanding it helps you make informed investment decisions.

Tips:

1. Research before investing—know the company and industry trends.
2. Avoid emotional decisions based on market fluctuations.
3. Start with index funds for broad exposure to the market.

Mindset Shift:
The stock market isn't a gamble—it's a tool for disciplined, informed investors to grow their wealth.

Quote:
"The stock market rewards patience and knowledge—invest wisely to reap its benefits."

44. The Basics of Mutual Funds and ETFs

Mutual funds pool money from many investors to buy a diversified portfolio of stocks, bonds, or other securities. ETFs (Exchange-Traded Funds) are similar but trade like stocks on an exchange. Both allow diversification without requiring you to select individual investments.

Why It Matters:

- Mutual funds and ETFs are great for beginners due to their simplicity and built-in diversification.
- They help reduce risk by spreading investments across multiple assets.

Tips:

1. Choose low-cost index funds or ETFs to minimize fees.
2. Research the fund's holdings and past performance.
3. Consider your investment goals and risk tolerance when selecting funds.

Mindset Shift:
Diversification is your safety net in investing—mutual funds and ETFs make it easy to spread risk.

Quote:
"Mutual funds and ETFs simplify investing—diversity is the foundation of stability."

45. Why Starting to Invest Early Matters

The earlier you start investing, the more time your money has to grow due to compound interest—earning returns on both your initial investment and previous gains. A small amount invested early can surpass a larger amount invested later.

Why It Matters:

- Time amplifies the power of compound interest.
- Starting early reduces the amount you need to save monthly to reach your goals.

Tips:

1. Invest as soon as you earn income, even if it's a small amount.
2. Focus on long-term growth rather than short-term fluctuations.
3. Take advantage of retirement accounts like IRAs or 401(k)s for tax benefits.

Mindset Shift:
Every year you delay investing costs you potential growth. Start now to make time your ally.

Quote:
"Invest early, invest often—time in the market beats timing the market."

46. The Concept of Risk vs. Reward

All investments involve risk, but higher risks often come with the potential for higher rewards. For example, stocks are riskier than bonds but offer higher long-term returns.

Why It Matters:

- Understanding risk helps you make informed investment decisions.
- Balancing risk and reward aligns your portfolio with your financial goals.

Tips:

1. Assess your risk tolerance—how much risk are you comfortable taking?
2. Diversify to spread risk across different asset types.
3. Avoid high-risk investments unless they align with your goals and timeline.

Mindset Shift:
Risk is part of the journey—understanding and managing it is the key to financial success.

Quote:
"Risk and reward go hand in hand—master the balance to achieve your financial dreams."

47. How to Research an Investment

Researching an investment involves analyzing its past performance, future growth potential, and associated risks. This includes studying financial statements, industry trends, and the overall economy.

Why It Matters:

- Informed decisions reduce the risk of losses.
- Research helps you align investments with your goals and values.

Tips:

1. Look at the company's earnings, debt, and growth potential.
2. Use tools like Morningstar or Yahoo Finance for analysis.
3. Read news and reports about the industry or asset type.

Mindset Shift:
Investing without research is like driving blindfolded—knowledge is your steering wheel.

Quote:
"Invest with knowledge, not emotion—research turns guesses into informed decisions."

48. The Power of Dollar-Cost Averaging

Dollar-cost averaging involves investing a fixed amount of money at regular intervals, regardless of market conditions. This strategy reduces the impact of market volatility by buying more shares when prices are low and fewer when prices are high.

Why It Matters:

- It minimizes the risk of investing a large sum at the wrong time.
- It promotes disciplined investing habits.

Tips:

1. Automate contributions to investment accounts.
2. Stay consistent, even during market downturns.
3. Focus on long-term growth rather than short-term fluctuations.

Mindset Shift:
Timing the market is nearly impossible—consistency is the key to steady growth.

Quote:
"Dollar-cost averaging makes the market's ups and downs work for you—invest steadily to win over time."

49. How to Diversify Your Investments

Diversification spreads your money across different asset types (e.g., stocks, bonds, real estate) and industries to reduce risk. A well-diversified portfolio is less likely to experience significant losses from any single investment.

Why It Matters:

- Reduces the impact of a poor-performing asset.
- Increases stability during market volatility.

Tips:

1. Invest in mutual funds or ETFs for easy diversification.
2. Balance your portfolio with a mix of high-risk and low-risk assets.
3. Review and adjust your portfolio regularly to maintain diversification.

Mindset Shift:
Don't put all your eggs in one basket—diversification is your safety net in uncertain markets.

Quote:
"Diversification isn't about avoiding risk—it's about managing it to build lasting wealth."

50. The Role of Dividends in Building Wealth

Dividends are payments companies make to shareholders from their profits. Reinvesting dividends allows your investment to grow faster through compounding, making them a powerful tool for wealth building.

Why It Matters:

- Dividends provide steady income even during market downturns.
- Reinvestment accelerates the growth of your portfolio.

Tips:

1. Invest in dividend-paying stocks or ETFs for long-term income.
2. Reinvest dividends automatically to maximize compounding.
3. Choose companies with a strong history of consistent dividend payments.

Mindset Shift:
Dividends are your money working for you—each payout is a step closer to financial independence.

Quote:
"Dividends are the rewards of patience—let them grow your wealth one payment at a time."

Chapter 5: Taxes

Taxes: Breaking It Down with the S.M.A.R.T. Approach

For young people just starting their financial journey, taxes can feel overwhelming, but they're an essential part of earning money and contributing to society. Taxes fund important services like schools, roads, healthcare, and emergency response. Whether you're working your first part-time job, freelancing, or just starting college, knowing how taxes work helps you avoid mistakes and keep more of your hard-earned money. Let's make it simple with the acronym S.M.A.R.T.:

- S: *Save for Taxes* – If you're earning freelance income or working gigs, taxes won't be automatically withheld like they are for most jobs. Set aside 20-30% of what you earn to cover your taxes when you file. This prevents any surprises come tax season.
- M: *Manage Your Documents* – Keep track of forms like the W-2 (for jobs) or 1099 (for gig or freelance work). Save receipts for school supplies, tuition, or other expenses that might qualify for tax deductions or credits. Staying organized is key.
- A: *Apply for Deductions and Credits* – Tax deductions lower the income you're taxed on, while credits directly

reduce your tax bill. For example, as a student, you might qualify for the American Opportunity Tax Credit or deductions for student loan interest. These can save you hundreds of dollars.
- R: *Review Your Pay Stub and Filing Status* – If you have a job, check your pay stub to see how much tax is being withheld. Use a W-4 form to adjust your withholdings if needed. Your filing status (single, dependent, etc.) also affects your tax rates, so make sure it's accurate.
- T: *Timely Filing* – File your taxes by the deadline (April 15 in the U.S.) to avoid late penalties. Tax software like TurboTax or FreeFile can walk you through the process, and many programs are free if you have simple taxes.

For many young people, taxes might seem intimidating, but they're manageable once you break them down. Whether you're earning from a part-time job, freelancing, or gig work, following the S.M.A.R.T. approach helps you stay on top of your tax obligations. The earlier you understand taxes, the more confident you'll feel managing your money and keeping as much of it in your pocket as possible. Taxes aren't just something you *have* to do—they're a way to plan for financial success.

51. Why Taxes Are a Part of Life

Taxes fund essential services like infrastructure, public education, healthcare, and national defense. Every time you earn income, make a purchase, or own property, taxes ensure that resources are available to maintain and improve societal systems.

Why It Matters:

- Understanding taxes helps you plan and budget effectively.
- Paying taxes contributes to the services and opportunities you rely on daily.

Tips:

1. Learn how different taxes (income, sales, property) impact your finances.
2. Use tools like tax calculators to estimate your liability.
3. Educate yourself on how taxes fund the public services you benefit from.

Mindset Shift:
Taxes aren't just a burden—they're a contribution to the society you live in.

Quote:
"Taxes are the price we pay for the benefits of a functioning society—understanding them empowers better financial choices."

52. The Basics of Income Tax Brackets

Income tax brackets determine how much you owe based on your taxable income. The U.S. uses a progressive tax system, meaning higher earnings are taxed at higher rates. Each portion of your income is taxed within its respective bracket.

Why It Matters:

- Knowing your tax bracket helps you plan deductions and credits effectively.
- Understanding how brackets work prevents overestimating your tax liability.

Tips:

1. Check current tax brackets for your filing status (e.g., single, married).
2. Use tax planning strategies to stay within lower brackets when possible.
3. Know that only the portion of income exceeding a bracket limit is taxed at the higher rate.

Mindset Shift:
Tax brackets don't punish success—they structure contributions fairly based on income.

Quote:
"Understanding tax brackets turns confusion into clarity—plan wisely to optimize your earnings."

---

53. How to File a Simple Tax Return

Filing a tax return involves reporting your income, deductions, and credits to calculate how much you owe or the refund you're entitled to. For a simple return, you'll need a W-2 form, your Social Security Number, and basic financial details.

Why It Matters:

- Filing accurately avoids penalties and ensures you receive any refunds due.
- Learning to file independently saves money on preparation fees.

Tips:

1. Use free e-filing tools if your income is below the threshold for paid services.
2. Double-check your entries to avoid errors that delay processing.
3. Keep copies of past returns for at least three years.

Mindset Shift:
Filing taxes is a responsibility, not a hassle—it's a chance to take control of your financial obligations.

Quote:
"Filing taxes is the final step in earning income responsibly—embrace it to stay on top of your financial game."

54. What a W-2 Form Is and How to Use It

A W-2 form is a document your employer provides annually, summarizing your earnings and taxes withheld during the year. It's essential for filing your tax return.

Why It Matters:

- The W-2 ensures accurate reporting of your income to the IRS.
- It helps you verify that enough taxes were withheld to avoid penalties.

Tips:

1. Check for accuracy—ensure your personal details and income amounts are correct.
2. Use the form to compare with your pay stubs throughout the year.
3. File your W-2 safely for future reference in case of audits.

Mindset Shift:
Your W-2 isn't just a piece of paper—it's a snapshot of your contributions and earnings.

Quote:
"Your W-2 is the foundation of your tax return—handle it with care to build a solid financial year."

55. How Deductions and Credits Reduce Taxes

Deductions lower your taxable income, while credits directly reduce the amount of tax you owe. For example, student loan interest is a deduction, while the Child Tax Credit directly reduces your tax bill.

Why It Matters:

- Deductions and credits can save you thousands of dollars annually.
- Knowing which ones you qualify for ensures you don't overpay.

Tips:

1. Research common deductions (e.g., mortgage interest, charitable donations) and credits (e.g., education or energy-saving credits).
2. Keep receipts and documentation to substantiate claims.
3. Use tax preparation software to identify eligible deductions and credits automatically.

Mindset Shift:
Deductions and credits aren't loopholes—they're incentives to support smart financial decisions.

Quote:
"Tax deductions and credits reward your financial choices—know them to keep more of what you earn."

56. The Importance of Keeping Tax Records

Tax records, including returns, receipts, and supporting documents, provide proof of your income and deductions in case of audits or discrepancies. The IRS recommends keeping records for at least three years.

Why It Matters:

- Records protect you during audits or disputes with the IRS.
- Organized records simplify future filings and financial planning.

Tips:

1. Use digital tools to store scanned copies of receipts and documents.
2. Label folders by tax year for easy retrieval.
3. Retain records for longer if they involve major transactions like home sales or investments.

Mindset Shift:
Keeping tax records isn't a chore—it's a safeguard for your financial integrity.

Quote:
"Well-kept records build a foundation of trust—stay organized to protect your financial future."

57. The Difference Between State and Federal Taxes

Federal taxes fund national programs like defense, healthcare, and Social Security, while state taxes support local services like education, transportation, and law enforcement. Not all states impose income tax, but they may have sales or property taxes.

Why It Matters:

- Understanding both helps you plan for your total tax liability.
- State tax rules can vary widely, impacting your financial strategy.

Tips:

1. Check your state's tax requirements for income, property, and sales taxes.
2. Consider state taxes when deciding where to live or work.
3. Use separate tools to calculate federal and state tax liabilities.

Mindset Shift:
State and federal taxes work together to fund services you use daily—understand both to plan better.

Quote:
"Taxes connect your contributions to your community—learn their purpose to maximize your impact."

58. How to Avoid Common Tax Scams

Tax scams often involve fraudulent emails, phone calls, or websites pretending to represent the IRS. Scammers aim to steal personal information or money by preying on fear of penalties.

Why It Matters:

- Protecting yourself from scams prevents identity theft and financial loss.
- Knowing IRS procedures helps you identify legitimate communications.

Tips:

1. Remember that the IRS never contacts you via email or phone—legitimate notices come by mail.
2. Don't share sensitive information unless you're sure of the source.
3. Use secure, reputable software for e-filing.

Mindset Shift:
Tax scams exploit fear—knowledge and vigilance keep your finances safe.

Quote:
"Awareness is your best defense against tax scams—stay informed to protect your identity and earnings."

59. Understanding the Importance of Tax Refunds

A tax refund occurs when you've paid more taxes than you owe during the year. While many view refunds as "bonus money," it's essentially an overpayment you're getting back.

Why It Matters:

- Receiving a refund indicates that too much was withheld from your paycheck.
- Adjusting withholdings lets you keep more of your money throughout the year.

Tips:

1. Use a W-4 form to adjust withholdings and reduce overpayment.
2. Save or invest refunds rather than treating them as extra spending money.
3. Avoid large refunds by managing your tax liability effectively.

Mindset Shift:
A tax refund isn't a windfall—it's a chance to redirect overpaid taxes toward your financial goals.

Quote:
"Your refund is your money—plan wisely to make it work for your future."

60. Why Paying Taxes on Time Is Crucial

Paying taxes on time avoids penalties, interest, and potential legal consequences. It also keeps your financial reputation intact with the IRS and creditors.

Why It Matters:

- Late payments incur fees and interest, increasing your overall liability.
- Delays can trigger audits or collection actions.

Tips:

1. Use reminders or automated systems to ensure timely payments.
2. If you can't pay in full, arrange a payment plan with the IRS.
3. File your return even if you can't pay immediately to minimize penalties.

Mindset Shift:
Timely tax payments reflect financial responsibility—avoid penalties by staying organized.

Quote:
"Paying taxes on time isn't just a duty—it's a step toward financial integrity and peace of mind."

Chapter 6: Mindset and Habits

Building Strong Money Habits

The habits you build around money now will set the tone for your financial future. Follow the acronym **S.A.V.E.R.** to guide your financial actions:

- S: *Set Goals* – Define clear financial goals, like saving for a car, college, or an emergency fund. Break them into smaller, manageable steps. For example, saving $1,200 in a year means putting aside $100 a month or about $25 a week.
- A: *Automate Savings* – If you have a bank account, set up an automatic transfer to savings whenever you get paid. Even small amounts add up over time.
- V: *Value Spending* – Spend money on what truly matters to you. Before buying something, ask yourself, *Does this align with my goals?* or *Will I still value this in a month?*
- E: *Educate Yourself* – Learn about budgeting, saving, and investing. Free apps like Mint or YNAB can help you track your money, while online resources can teach you about managing finances.

- R: *Review and Reflect* – Regularly check in with your budget and progress. Celebrate small wins, like hitting a savings milestone, to stay motivated.

Start Small, Think Big

Good financial habits don't have to start with big numbers. If you earn money from an allowance, part-time job, or side hustle, begin by saving 10-20% of what you make. Set up a separate savings account or even use an envelope system to keep your savings untouched. Track your spending for a week or two to see where your money is going—you might be surprised how small changes, like skipping an unnecessary purchase, can boost your savings.

The Long-Term Impact

The earlier you start building smart financial habits, the more time your money has to grow. For example, saving $50 a month starting at age 18 and investing it in a simple index fund earning 7% annually could grow to over $100,000 by age 50. Starting at 25 instead of 18 could cut that amount in half. This is the power of *compound interest*, where your savings earn interest, and that interest earns even more interest over time.

Final Thoughts

Your mindset and habits with money now are laying the groundwork for financial freedom. By adopting the S.A.V.E.R. framework, practicing intentional spending, and starting small, you'll build confidence in managing your finances and achieve your goals faster than you think. Remember, every dollar you save or invest today is an investment in your future. The sooner you start, the bigger the impact will be. You've got this!

61. Why a Positive Money Mindset Is Essential

A positive money mindset involves viewing money as a tool to achieve goals rather than as a source of stress or limitation. This mindset encourages growth, confidence, and the belief that financial success is attainable.

Why It Matters:

- A healthy attitude toward money reduces financial stress.
- It fosters motivation to make smarter financial decisions.

Tips:

1. Replace negative thoughts like "I'll never have enough" with affirmations like "I'm working toward abundance."
2. Focus on opportunities for growth rather than financial obstacles.
3. Surround yourself with people and resources that encourage a positive outlook on finances.

Mindset Shift:
Money is a tool, not a measure of your worth. Treat it as a partner in achieving your dreams.

Quote:
"A positive money mindset transforms financial challenges into opportunities for growth."

62. The Power of Delayed Gratification

Delayed gratification means resisting the temptation of immediate rewards in favor of long-term gains. It's a cornerstone of financial success, helping you save, invest, and achieve meaningful goals.

Why It Matters:

- It prevents impulse spending and fosters disciplined saving.
- Sacrificing small pleasures today leads to greater rewards tomorrow.

Tips:

1. Set clear goals to stay motivated while delaying gratification.
2. Use the "24-hour rule" for non-essential purchases.
3. Reward yourself periodically to balance discipline with enjoyment.

Mindset Shift:
Patience is the currency of success—delaying gratification is how you buy your dreams.

Quote:
"Great rewards come to those who wait—delayed gratification turns patience into prosperity."

63. How Gratitude Can Shift Your Financial Outlook

Gratitude shifts your focus from what you lack to what you have, fostering contentment and reducing the urge to overspend. It helps you appreciate your financial journey, no matter the stage.

Why It Matters:
- Gratitude combats the comparison trap and promotes mindful spending.
- It inspires generosity and a sense of abundance.

Tips:
1. Write down three financial blessings daily, like a steady job or a paid-off debt.
2. Celebrate small victories, such as sticking to your budget.
3. Volunteer or give back to others to cultivate gratitude for your own financial position.

Mindset Shift:
Gratitude is the key to contentment—it transforms what you have into enough.

Quote:
"Gratitude turns your financial focus from scarcity to abundance, revealing the wealth you already possess."

64. The Importance of Self-Discipline with Money

Self-discipline is the ability to control spending, stick to a budget, and prioritize long-term goals over instant gratification. It's a skill that protects you from financial pitfalls and builds wealth over time.

Why It Matters:

- Discipline helps you avoid debt and save consistently.
- It ensures you stay on track toward financial goals.

Tips:

1. Automate savings to reduce the temptation to spend.
2. Create a spending plan that includes both needs and small indulgences.
3. Practice saying "no" to unplanned purchases.

Mindset Shift:
Self-discipline isn't restrictive—it's liberating. It empowers you to take control of your financial destiny.

Quote:
"Discipline is the bridge between goals and financial freedom."

65. Why Failure Is Part of Financial Success

Failure is a natural part of any journey, including finances. Mistakes like overspending, investing poorly, or missing goals offer valuable lessons that pave the way for long-term success.

Why It Matters:

- Learning from financial missteps prevents repeated errors.
- Overcoming failure builds resilience and confidence.

Tips:

1. Reflect on financial mistakes to identify what went wrong.
2. Focus on solutions instead of dwelling on the problem.
3. Use setbacks as motivation to improve your financial habits.

Mindset Shift:
Failure isn't the opposite of success—it's a stepping stone toward it.

Quote:
"Every financial misstep is a lesson in disguise—embrace failure as a guide to success."

66. How to Set SMART Financial Goals

SMART financial goals are Specific, Measurable, Achievable, Relevant, and Time-bound. For example, instead of "save money," set a goal like "save $5,000 for an emergency fund in 12 months."

Why It Matters:

- Clear goals provide direction and motivation.
- SMART goals break big ambitions into manageable steps.

Tips:

1. Write down your goals and track progress regularly.
2. Prioritize goals by importance and urgency.
3. Adjust timelines or strategies as needed to stay realistic.

Mindset Shift:
Financial success starts with clarity—SMART goals give your dreams a blueprint.

Quote:
"Goals without plans are just wishes—SMART goals turn aspirations into achievements."

---

67. The Importance of Continuous Financial Education

The financial world evolves constantly, and staying informed ensures you can adapt and make better decisions. Whether it's learning about new investment opportunities or tax strategies, knowledge is key to financial growth.

Why It Matters:

- It helps you avoid outdated practices and take advantage of new opportunities.
- Financial literacy improves decision-making and builds confidence.

Tips:

1. Read books, blogs, or articles about personal finance regularly.
2. Take courses or attend workshops on budgeting, investing, or debt management.
3. Follow reputable financial experts for insights and trends.

Mindset Shift:
Money mastery is a journey, not a destination. Every lesson brings you closer to financial independence.

Quote:
"Continuous learning keeps your financial skills sharp and your goals within reach."

68. Why Comparing Yourself to Others Can Hurt Your Finances

Comparing your financial situation to others often leads to unnecessary spending, debt, or feelings of inadequacy. Everyone's financial journey is unique, shaped by different goals and circumstances.

Why It Matters:

- Comparison fosters unhealthy habits like keeping up with appearances.
- It distracts you from focusing on your own progress.

Tips:

1. Celebrate your achievements, no matter how small.
2. Focus on personal goals rather than external benchmarks.
3. Limit exposure to social media or environments that trigger comparison.

Mindset Shift:
Your financial journey is your own—comparison robs you of the joy and progress you've earned.

Quote:
"Comparison steals contentment—focus on your own growth to achieve financial peace."

69. How Small, Consistent Steps Lead to Big Results

Consistent actions, like saving a small amount regularly or making tiny budget adjustments, compound over time to create significant outcomes. It's the principle behind habits like investing early or reducing debt incrementally.

Why It Matters:

- Small habits are sustainable and lead to lasting change.
- Consistency builds momentum and confidence.

Tips:

1. Set small, achievable milestones to maintain motivation.
2. Automate savings or debt payments to ensure regular progress.
3. Track your progress to see how small actions add up over time.

Mindset Shift:
Success isn't about grand gestures—it's about small, consistent steps taken daily.

Quote:
"Big achievements are built on small, steady efforts—every step counts."

70. The Value of Celebrating Financial Milestones

Celebrating milestones, like paying off a debt or reaching a savings goal, reinforces positive behavior and keeps you motivated. It's a way to acknowledge your hard work and progress.

Why It Matters:

- Celebrations create emotional rewards for disciplined financial habits.
- They keep you energized for the next goal.

Tips:

1. Choose rewards that don't derail your progress, like a small treat or experience.
2. Share your successes with supportive friends or family.
3. Use each milestone celebration to set your sights on the next goal.

Mindset Shift:
Every financial win, no matter how small, is worth celebrating—it's proof of your effort and growth.

Quote:
"Celebrate your progress—it's the fuel that powers your journey to financial success."

Chapter 7: Entrepreneurship

Entrepreneurship is an exciting way for you to explore creativity, earn money, and build valuable skills for the future. Whether it's starting a small business, a side hustle, or launching a digital service, turning ideas into income teaches you independence and problem-solving. Use the acronym **S.T.A.R.T.** to guide your journey.

First, **See Opportunities** by identifying problems you can solve or gaps in the market, like affordable tutoring or creating custom art.

Then, **Take Action** by starting small—create a product, offer a service, or promote your idea on social media.

Remember to **Adapt and Learn** through trial and error; if something doesn't work, figure out why and adjust your approach while gaining new skills like marketing or budgeting.

Next, **Reach Your Audience** by connecting with people who need your product or service. Use social media or local networks to showcase your work and engage potential customers.

Finally, **Think Long-Term** by planning for growth, whether it's reinvesting your earnings, adding new products, or scaling your business. Starting young allows you to experiment, learn, and build something meaningful without as much pressure. Whether you're freelancing, selling handmade crafts, or offering tech help, your efforts today can lead to financial independence and opportunities for the future. Entrepreneurship is all about action, creativity, and persistence—take the first step now and see where your ideas can take you!

71. How to Identify a Business Idea

Identifying a business idea starts with understanding your passions, skills, and the problems you can solve for others. A strong business idea lies at the intersection of what you love, what you're good at, and what the market needs. It's important to validate your idea to ensure it has demand and the potential for profitability.

Why It Matters:

- A clear and well-thought-out idea reduces the risk of failure.
- It provides focus and direction for your entrepreneurial journey.
- Starting with the right idea increases the likelihood of long-term success.

Tips:

1. **Identify Problems:** Look for pain points in your daily life or in industries that interest you.
2. **Research Demand:** Use tools like Google Trends or social media platforms to see if others are discussing the problem.
3. **Validate the Idea:** Create a small prototype or service test and gather feedback from potential customers.
4. **Leverage Your Skills:** Build a business around your strengths to increase confidence and efficiency.

Mindset Shift:
Think of your business as a solution provider. The better you address people's needs, the more successful your business will be.

Quote:
"Every great business starts with a simple question: What problem can I solve for others?"

72. The Basics of Creating a Business Plan

A business plan is a document that outlines your business goals, target audience, strategies, and financial projections. It acts as a roadmap, guiding your decisions and keeping you on track. A good plan also communicates your vision to investors, partners, and employees.

Why It Matters:

- A business plan helps clarify your vision and set measurable goals.
- It forces you to think critically about your strategy and resources.
- It's often required to secure loans or attract investors.

Tips:

1. **Executive Summary:** Start with a concise overview of your business, mission, and goals.
2. **Market Research:** Analyze your target audience, competitors, and industry trends.
3. **Financial Projections:** Include realistic estimates for revenue, expenses, and profitability.
4. **Marketing and Sales Strategy:** Detail how you plan to attract and retain customers.

Mindset Shift:
Your business plan isn't just a formality—it's a living document that evolves with your business.

Quote:
"A well-crafted business plan is the compass that keeps your entrepreneurial ship on course."

73. Understanding Profit and Loss

Profit is the revenue left after all expenses are paid, while a **Profit and Loss (P&L) statement** tracks income, expenses, and net profit over a specific period. This essential financial tool helps you understand your business's financial health.

Why It Matters:

- Shows whether your business is profitable or needs adjustments.
- Helps identify areas where you can cut costs or increase revenue.
- Provides data for tax preparation and investor reporting.

Tips:

1. **Track Everything:** Record all income and expenses using accounting software like QuickBooks or Wave.
2. **Analyze Trends:** Review P&L statements monthly to spot patterns in income and spending.
3. **Understand Key Metrics:** Learn terms like gross profit, net profit, and operating expenses to interpret your P&L effectively.
4. **Cut Waste:** Use the P&L to identify and eliminate unnecessary expenses.

Mindset Shift:
Profit isn't just the end goal—it's a measure of how well you manage your business.

Quote:
"Understanding profit and loss isn't just about money—it's about mastering the financial pulse of your business."

74. How to Market a Small Business

Marketing involves creating awareness about your products or services and convincing potential customers to choose you over competitors. For small businesses, marketing often relies on creativity and understanding your target audience rather than a massive budget.

Why It Matters:

- Attracts new customers and retains existing ones.
- Helps differentiate your business in a competitive market.
- Builds your brand and establishes trust.

Tips:

1. **Define Your Audience:** Understand who your ideal customers are, their needs, and how to reach them.
2. **Leverage Social Media:** Use platforms like Instagram, Facebook, or LinkedIn to engage with your audience.
3. **Focus on Content Marketing:** Create valuable content (e.g., blogs, videos) to educate and attract customers.
4. **Track ROI:** Use analytics tools to measure the effectiveness of your campaigns and adjust strategies accordingly.

Mindset Shift:
Marketing isn't about selling—it's about connecting with your audience and showing them how your business improves their lives.

Quote:
"Great marketing doesn't interrupt—it inspires and connects."

75. The Importance of Customer Service

Customer service refers to how you interact with your customers to meet or exceed their expectations. Exceptional service is a key differentiator, particularly for small businesses.

Why It Matters:

- Builds trust and loyalty, leading to repeat business.
- Positive experiences encourage referrals and word-of-mouth marketing.
- Poor customer service can damage your reputation and drive customers away.

Tips:

1. **Listen Actively:** Make customers feel heard by addressing their concerns promptly.
2. **Train Your Team:** Equip employees with the skills and knowledge to deliver excellent service.
3. **Go the Extra Mile:** Small gestures, like follow-up emails or personalized thank-yous, make a big difference.
4. **Respond Quickly:** Aim to resolve issues as soon as possible to maintain customer satisfaction.

Mindset Shift:
Customer service isn't just an interaction—it's the foundation of trust and loyalty.

Quote:
"Exceptional service turns customers into ambassadors for your brand."

76. How to Manage Business Expenses

Managing expenses involves tracking, controlling, and optimizing your spending to ensure profitability. This includes fixed costs like rent and variable costs like marketing or inventory.

Why It Matters:

- Proper expense management ensures healthy cash flow.
- Helps avoid unnecessary debt and improve profit margins.
- Allows you to allocate resources efficiently for growth.

Tips:

1. **Separate Finances:** Open a dedicated business bank account to keep personal and business expenses separate.
2. **Track Spending:** Use software like Expensify or Wave to monitor and categorize expenses.
3. **Cut Unnecessary Costs:** Regularly review spending to identify areas for savings.
4. **Negotiate Contracts:** Work with vendors to secure better terms or discounts.

Mindset Shift:
Managing expenses isn't about cutting corners—it's about maximizing the value of every dollar spent.

Quote:
"Every dollar saved is a dollar reinvested in your business's future."

77. The Basics of Registering a Business

Registering your business is the process of legally establishing it under your chosen name and structure (e.g., LLC, sole proprietorship). This step protects your personal assets and ensures compliance with local, state, and federal regulations.

Why It Matters:

- Legitimizes your business and builds trust with customers.
- Protects your personal assets in case of legal or financial issues.
- Provides access to business loans and tax benefits.

Tips:

1. **Choose the Right Structure:** Decide between options like LLC, corporation, or sole proprietorship based on your needs.
2. **Register Your Name:** Ensure your business name is unique and secure a domain for your website.
3. **Obtain Permits:** Research and acquire any licenses or permits required in your industry.

Mindset Shift:
Registering your business is more than legal paperwork—it's the first step in building your brand's credibility.

Quote:
"Registering your business transforms your idea into a recognized and protected entity."

78. Understanding the Role of Taxes in Business

Business taxes include income taxes, payroll taxes, and sales taxes. Proper tax management ensures compliance, avoids penalties, and maximizes deductions to reduce liability.

Why It Matters:

- Keeps your business in good standing with tax authorities.
- Helps you avoid fines or legal issues due to non-compliance.
- Reduces your overall tax burden through deductions and credits.

Tips:

1. **Track Expenses:** Keep detailed records of deductible costs like travel, office supplies, and advertising.
2. **Hire a Professional:** Work with a tax accountant to navigate complex regulations.
3. **File on Time:** Use reminders or automated tools to ensure timely payments and filings.

Mindset Shift:
Taxes aren't just an obligation—they're a part of running a responsible, successful business.

Quote:
"Managing taxes isn't just compliance—it's a strategic part of financial planning."

79. The Value of Networking for Growth

Networking involves building relationships with other professionals to share knowledge, find opportunities, and collaborate on projects. A strong network accelerates growth by connecting you to resources and new markets.

Why It Matters:

- Expands your reach and increases your visibility.
- Opens doors to partnerships, funding, and mentorship.

Tips:

1. **Attend Events:** Join industry conferences, trade shows, or local business groups.
2. **Leverage Social Media:** Use platforms like LinkedIn to connect with professionals in your field.
3. **Be Authentic:** Focus on building genuine relationships, not just transactional connections.

Mindset Shift:
Networking isn't just about who you know—it's about how you contribute and collaborate.

Quote:
"Your network is your business's backbone—strong relationships lead to lasting success."

80. Why Resilience Is Critical in Entrepreneurship

Resilience is the ability to recover from setbacks and keep going in the face of challenges. It's a necessary trait for entrepreneurs who face uncertainty, competition, and risk.

Why It Matters:
- Helps you adapt to changes and overcome obstacles.
- Builds confidence to persist through tough times.

Tips:
1. **Focus on Solutions:** Instead of dwelling on problems, brainstorm actionable steps to move forward.
2. **Learn from Setbacks:** Treat failures as learning opportunities to refine your strategies.
3. **Build a Support System:** Surround yourself with mentors, peers, and friends who encourage and guide you.

Mindset Shift:
Resilience isn't just about bouncing back—it's about growing stronger with each challenge.

Quote:
"Resilience transforms challenges into stepping stones—every setback is a setup for success."

Chapter 8: Spending Wisely

Spending wisely between the ages of 14 and 25 is like embarking on a treasure hunt—every financial decision you make is a step closer to achieving your dreams. Whether you're earning money from a part-time job, freelancing, or an allowance, how you choose to spend will determine the strength of your financial foundation. It's not about never enjoying your money; it's about spending with purpose and making sure every dollar works for you. By adopting the **G.O.L.D.** framework, you can build smart habits and avoid common spending pitfalls. Here's how **G.O.L.D.** can guide you:

- **G**: *Gauge the Value* – Before spending, ask yourself, *Is this worth my money?* Prioritize items or experiences that add long-term value, such as a good pair of shoes that last years or a course that enhances your skills.
- **O**: *Optimize Your Spending* – Stretch your dollars by looking for deals, discounts, or smarter alternatives. Take advantage of student discounts, sales, or free versions of tools and services when possible.
- **L**: *Limit Impulse Buys* – Avoid the temptation to buy on a whim by practicing the "24-hour rule." Wait a day before making non-essential purchases, and you'll often find you didn't really need or want it.

- **D**: *Direct Funds to Goals* – Treat your money like a ship heading toward your dreams. Allocate spending to things that align with your priorities, like saving for college, a car, or a big trip.

Learning to gauge value means looking beyond the immediate thrill of a purchase and considering whether it aligns with your long-term goals. This mindset helps you avoid wasting money on items you'll quickly forget about. For instance, a trendy gadget might feel exciting now but lose its appeal in a few weeks, while investing in quality gear or a skill can have lasting benefits. Optimizing spending involves finding creative ways to make your money go further, like buying second hand, splitting costs with friends, or taking advantage of promotions.

Limiting impulse buys can be challenging, especially with the ease of online shopping, but it's one of the best ways to protect your finances. By pausing to reflect before making a purchase, you give yourself time to decide whether it truly matters to you. Finally, directing funds toward meaningful goals keeps you on track to achieve the things that matter most, whether it's saving for a specific item, building an emergency fund, or planning for a memorable experience.

Spending wisely doesn't mean depriving yourself of fun or enjoyment—it's about spending intentionally. Budget for the things you love, like hobbies, entertainment, or dining out with friends, while ensuring you're also investing in your future. By following the **G.O.L.D.** framework, you'll not only manage your money better but also feel more in control of your financial journey. Each thoughtful choice you make today will lead to a future filled with opportunities and success.

81. How to Compare Prices Before Buying

Price comparison ensures you get the best deal on a product or service. With online tools and apps, it's easier than ever to compare prices across multiple retailers.

Why It Matters:

- Saves money by identifying the lowest price for the same product.
- Helps you evaluate whether a sale or deal is truly worth it.

Tips:

1. Use price comparison websites or apps like Honey or Google Shopping.
2. Check both in-store and online prices for potential savings.
3. Factor in shipping costs and taxes when comparing prices.

Mindset Shift:
Smart shopping isn't about spending less—it's about spending wisely.

Quote:
"Comparing prices is like finding hidden treasure—it ensures every dollar is spent with purpose."

82. The Importance of Reading Product Reviews

Product reviews provide insight into the quality, usability, and reliability of an item before you buy. Honest feedback from other buyers can help you make an informed decision.

Why It Matters:

- Avoids wasting money on low-quality or unsuitable products.
- Highlights potential issues you might not have considered.

Tips:

1. Read both positive and negative reviews to get a balanced view.
2. Look for reviews with photos or detailed experiences for authenticity.
3. Be cautious of fake reviews—cross-check feedback across multiple platforms.

Mindset Shift:
Reviews are the experiences of others paving the way for smarter decisions.

Quote:
"Trust the wisdom of others—reviews save you from learning costly lessons the hard way."

83. How to Avoid Impulse Purchases

Impulse purchases happen when you buy something without planning, often driven by emotions or marketing tactics. Avoiding them ensures your money is spent on priorities.

Why It Matters:

- Prevents overspending and buyer's remorse.
- Helps you stick to your financial goals.

Tips:

1. Use the 24-hour rule: Wait a day before making non-essential purchases.
2. Create a shopping list and stick to it.
3. Unsubscribe from marketing emails that encourage impulsive buys.

Mindset Shift:
Impulse purchases satisfy for a moment, but intentional spending creates lasting value.

Quote:
"Pause before you purchase—intentional choices lead to financial freedom."

84. Why Buying Quality Can Save Money Long-Term

Investing in high-quality items often costs more upfront but saves money over time by reducing replacements or repairs. Quality over quantity is a principle that applies to clothing, appliances, and more.

Why It Matters:

- Durable products last longer and provide better value.
- Saves time and stress associated with frequent replacements.

Tips:

1. Research brands known for quality and durability.
2. Read reviews to confirm long-term satisfaction with the product.
3. Apply the cost-per-use calculation to evaluate the true value of an item.

Mindset Shift:
Buying quality isn't an expense—it's an investment in reliability and peace of mind.

Quote:
"Quality pays for itself over time—choose well, and you'll save more in the long run."

85. How to Use Coupons and Discounts

Coupons and discounts are valuable tools for saving money on everyday purchases. Whether through apps, websites, or loyalty programs, they can significantly reduce your expenses.

Why It Matters:

- Stretch your budget further by reducing costs on essentials.
- Encourages smarter spending habits.

Tips:

1. Use apps like Rakuten, RetailMeNot, or Honey to find discounts automatically.
2. Combine coupons with sales for maximum savings.
3. Sign up for store loyalty programs to access exclusive deals.

Mindset Shift:
Using coupons isn't about being cheap—it's about being resourceful.

Quote:
"Every dollar saved is a dollar earned—coupons and discounts are your financial allies."

86. The Value of Waiting for Sales

Waiting for sales allows you to purchase items at a fraction of their regular cost. Planning your purchases around seasonal or annual sales events can save significant money.

Why It Matters:

- Maximizes your purchasing power.
- Reduces the guilt or regret of paying full price.

Tips:

1. Mark sales events like Black Friday, Cyber Monday, or end-of-season clearances.
2. Use wishlists to track items you want and wait for price drops.
3. Be patient—most products go on sale within a few months.

Mindset Shift:
Patience turns wants into smart purchases, making your money work harder for you.

Quote:
"Good things come to those who wait—and sales make those things even better."

87. How to Identify and Avoid Scams

Scams often target unsuspecting buyers with fake deals or counterfeit products. Knowing how to spot red flags ensures you avoid financial loss and protect your personal information.

Why It Matters:

- Protects your hard-earned money and identity.
- Helps maintain trust in online and in-store purchases.

Tips:

1. Verify seller credibility through reviews and ratings.
2. Avoid deals that seem too good to be true.
3. Use secure payment methods, like credit cards, for additional protection.

Mindset Shift:
Caution isn't paranoia—it's protection for your financial and personal security.

Quote:
"Vigilance turns potential scams into opportunities for smarter, safer spending."

88. The Importance of Researching Major Purchases

Major purchases, like appliances, electronics, or cars, require careful research to ensure you get the best value for your money. Rushing into these decisions can lead to regret or unnecessary costs.

Why It Matters:

- Ensures your investment meets your needs and expectations.
- Helps you avoid buyer's remorse.

Tips:

1. Compare features, warranties, and prices across brands.
2. Test or view the product in person, if possible, before buying.
3. Read expert reviews and customer feedback for well-rounded insights.

Mindset Shift:
Research is the price of confidence—invest time upfront to enjoy your purchase longer.

Quote:
"A well-researched purchase is never a gamble—it's a calculated investment."

89. The Benefits of Shopping Second-Hand

Buying second-hand items like clothing, furniture, or electronics offers significant savings while supporting sustainability. Thrift stores, consignment shops, and online marketplaces make it easy to find quality items at a fraction of the cost.

Why It Matters:

- Saves money while reducing waste.
- Offers unique finds that may no longer be available.

Tips:

1. Inspect items for quality and functionality before purchasing.
2. Use platforms like eBay, Poshmark, or Facebook Marketplace.
3. Negotiate prices when possible to maximize savings.

Mindset Shift:
Second-hand isn't second-best—it's a smart way to save money and reduce your environmental impact.

Quote:
"Shopping second-hand turns thrift into triumph—save money while making a difference."

90. How to Calculate the True Cost of Ownership

The true cost of ownership includes not just the purchase price but also ongoing expenses like maintenance, repairs, energy use, and depreciation. Understanding this helps you make smarter financial decisions.

Why It Matters:

- Prevents underestimating the long-term costs of a purchase.
- Helps you evaluate whether an item is worth its price.

Tips:

1. Factor in maintenance costs, like fuel for a car or energy usage for appliances.
2. Compare long-term expenses between different brands or models.
3. Choose products with warranties or low-cost maintenance to reduce total costs.

Mindset Shift:
The price tag doesn't tell the whole story—look deeper to see the real cost.

Quote:
"The true cost of ownership is the price you pay for convenience—know it before you commit."

Chapter 9: Insurance and Protection

Insurance and Protection: Preparing for the Unexpected

While you are young, insurance might not feel like something you need to worry about yet. For many people in this age range, parents are still handling things like health insurance, car insurance, and even renter's insurance if you're living at home or in a dorm. However, understanding how insurance works now gives you the knowledge to make informed decisions when the time comes to manage it on your own. Think of insurance as a financial safety net—one that protects you from the high costs of unexpected events like medical emergencies, accidents, or theft. Knowing the basics now is empowering, so you're ready when those responsibilities shift to you.

What Is Insurance?

Insurance is essentially a financial agreement between you and an insurance company. You pay a regular fee, called a **premium**, and in return, the insurance company helps cover costs if something goes wrong. This could include paying for medical bills, repairing a car, or replacing stolen belongings. Without insurance, you'd have to pay the full amount out of pocket, which can be overwhelming. By sharing the risk, insurance ensures you're not financially devastated by unexpected events.

Types of Insurance You'll Encounter

Most young people will encounter a few key types of insurance, often managed by their parents. Here's what they are and why they matter:

- **Health Insurance**: Covers medical costs like doctor visits, prescriptions, and hospital stays. While you're likely on your parents' plan until 26 (in the U.S.), you'll need to understand how to choose a plan later, whether through work or individually.
- **Car Insurance**: If you drive, car insurance is typically required by law. It covers damages and injuries caused by accidents, theft, or natural disasters. Even if you're on your parents' policy now, one day you'll need to manage your own.
- **Renter's Insurance**: Protects your belongings in a dorm, apartment, or rental house from theft or damage. If your laptop gets stolen or your dorm floods, renter's

insurance covers the costs. This is often overlooked but incredibly valuable.
- **Life Insurance**: While not urgent now, life insurance becomes important if you have dependents in the future or want to lock in affordable rates while you're young.
- **Disability Insurance**: Replaces a portion of your income if you're unable to work due to illness or injury. This is especially helpful as you begin working and become financially independent.

Why Should You Care Now?

Even though your parents might handle these responsibilities now, understanding insurance is a crucial step toward independence. The choices you make in your mid-to-late 20s—like moving out, buying a car, or starting a job—will require you to navigate insurance on your own. Knowing the basics now means you'll be confident when the time comes. Use the acronym **S.H.I.E.L.D.** to remember how insurance protects you and what you should know:

- **S**: *Stay Covered* – Insurance ensures you're financially protected from major costs, whether it's a car accident or medical emergency.

- **H**: *Handle Unexpected Costs* – Accidents and surprises happen; insurance helps you manage those without derailing your finances.
- **I**: *Invest in Security* – Paying a small premium now protects you from much larger expenses later.
- **E**: *Educate Yourself* – Learn what policies cover and how they work so you can make informed decisions when you need to choose your own.
- **L**: *Lower Financial Risk* – Insurance minimizes your out-of-pocket expenses in high-cost situations.
- **D**: *Develop Good Habits* – Understanding insurance now builds skills for managing your financial responsibilities in the future.

How to Prepare for Managing Insurance

While you may not need to handle insurance yet, there are steps you can take to prepare for the future:

1. **Ask Questions**: Talk to your parents about the types of insurance they have for you and why. Understanding how it works gives you a foundation for managing it later.

2. **Track Basics**: Learn what premiums, deductibles, and coverage limits mean. This will help you compare policies when the time comes.
3. **Start Small**: If you live in a dorm or apartment, consider getting renter's insurance. It's affordable and teaches you how to manage a policy.
4. **Pay Attention to Changes**: As you transition to independence—getting a full-time job, buying a car, or moving out—insurance will become a necessary part of those decisions.

Final Thoughts

At this stage of life, your parents are likely handling your insurance needs, but the day will come when these responsibilities are yours. Learning about insurance now isn't just about being prepared—it's about gaining the confidence to manage your financial future. Whether it's understanding health insurance options, knowing why renter's insurance matters, or planning for car insurance costs, building this knowledge now gives you a head start. Remember, insurance isn't just an expense—it's a *S.H.I.E.L.D.*

that protects your financial stability and ensures peace of mind when life's unexpected events occur.

91. The Basics of Health, Auto, Renters, and Life Insurance

- **Health Insurance**: Covers medical expenses, preventive care, and treatments to reduce out-of-pocket costs for illnesses or injuries.
- **Auto Insurance**: Protects against financial loss due to accidents, theft, or vehicle damage. Liability coverage is often legally required.
- **Renters Insurance**: Covers your personal belongings and provides liability protection if you rent a home or apartment.
- **Life Insurance**: Provides financial support to your loved ones in the event of your passing, covering expenses like debts, income replacement, and funeral costs.

Why It Matters:

- Insurance helps manage risks and prevents financial hardship from unexpected events.
- Health and auto insurance are crucial for personal protection and often legally required.
- Life insurance ensures your loved ones are financially secure in your absence.

Tips:

1. **Understand Coverage**: Review what each policy covers and excludes, ensuring it fits your specific needs.

2. **Choose the Right Policies**: Start with essentials like health, auto, and renters insurance, and add life insurance for long-term planning.
3. **Annual Reviews**: Regularly assess your policies to ensure they remain adequate as your life circumstances change.

Mindset Shift: Insurance isn't an expense—it's a safeguard for your health, finances, and loved ones.

"Insurance turns life's uncertainties into manageable risks—invest in peace of mind for yourself and those who depend on you."

92. Why Insurance Is a Form of Financial Protection

Insurance transfers financial risk from you to the insurer, covering costs for major life events like illness, accidents, or natural disasters. Without it, you might face significant financial setbacks.

Why It Matters:

- Reduces stress by preparing for the unexpected.
- Ensures you're not left financially vulnerable in a crisis.

Tips:

1. Prioritize insurance for health, auto, home, and life before considering extras.
2. Use a licensed insurance agent to help identify your specific needs.
3. Consider bundling policies (e.g., auto and renters) for discounts.

Mindset Shift:
Insurance isn't an expense—it's an investment in peace of mind and financial stability.

Quote:
"Insurance doesn't prevent risks, but it protects you from their worst financial consequences."

93. How Deductibles and Premiums Work

- A premium is the amount you pay for insurance coverage, often monthly or annually.
- A deductible is the amount you must pay out-of-pocket before the insurer covers the remaining costs.

Why It Matters:

- Understanding these terms helps you choose the right balance of affordability and coverage.
- Higher deductibles usually mean lower premiums and vice versa.

Tips:
1. Choose a deductible you can comfortably afford in an emergency.
2. Compare policies with different deductible and premium options to find the best value.
3. Set aside an emergency fund to cover deductibles if needed.

Mindset Shift:
Your premium is your upfront protection, and your deductible is your financial buffer—understand both to make smart choices.

Quote:
"Deductibles and premiums define the balance between risk and readiness—know your numbers to stay prepared."

94. The Importance of Comparing Insurance Quotes

Comparing quotes ensures you're getting the best coverage at the most affordable price. Different insurers offer varying rates for the same coverage based on factors like age, location, and driving record.

Why It Matters:

- Saves money by identifying better deals.
- Helps you avoid overpaying for unnecessary coverage.

Tips:

1. Use online tools like Policygenius or Zebra to compare multiple quotes.
2. Reassess your insurance every 1-2 years to ensure you're still getting the best rate.
3. Look beyond price—consider customer service and claims satisfaction ratings.

Mindset Shift:
Insurance isn't one-size-fits-all—comparison shopping tailors coverage to your needs and budget.

Quote:
"Comparing insurance quotes ensures your peace of mind doesn't come at an unnecessary cost."

95. How to File an Insurance Claim

Filing a claim involves notifying your insurer about a covered event and requesting compensation or coverage for damages or losses. Proper documentation speeds up the process.

Why It Matters:

- Knowing the process ensures you receive benefits promptly in times of need.
- Prevents delays caused by missing paperwork or incomplete information.

Tips:

1. Document the incident with photos, videos, and detailed descriptions.
2. Contact your insurer immediately after the event.
3. Follow up regularly to ensure timely processing.

Mindset Shift:
A claim isn't just paperwork—it's your right to the protection you've paid for.

Quote:
"Filing a claim is the moment your insurance works for you—prepare to make the process seamless."

96. The Role of Life Insurance in Long-Term Planning

Life insurance provides financial support to your loved ones in the event of your passing. It can cover expenses like debts, funeral costs, and income replacement, ensuring your family's financial stability.

Why It Matters:

- Protects your dependents from financial hardship.
- Serves as a tool for wealth transfer and estate planning.

Tips:

1. Determine how much coverage you need based on your debts, income, and family's future expenses.
2. Consider term life insurance for affordability or whole life insurance for lifelong coverage.
3. Review your policy every few years to ensure it meets your current needs.

Mindset Shift:
Life insurance isn't for you—it's a gift of security and stability for your loved ones.

"Life insurance turns your legacy into a shield for your family's future."

97. Why Identity Theft Protection Matters

Identity theft protection services monitor your personal information and alert you to suspicious activity. They help minimize damage and provide assistance if your identity is stolen.

Why It Matters:

- Identity theft can lead to financial losses, damaged credit, and legal issues.
- Early detection reduces the impact of fraudulent activity.

Tips:

1. Use services like LifeLock or IdentityForce to monitor your accounts.
2. Regularly review your bank and credit card statements for unauthorized transactions.
3. Freeze your credit if you suspect fraud or identity theft.

Mindset Shift:
Protecting your identity is as important as protecting your wallet—both are keys to your financial health.

"Identity theft protection is an investment in peace of mind—your identity is your most valuable asset."

98. How to Recognize Phishing Scams

Phishing scams use fake emails, messages, or websites to steal sensitive information like passwords or credit card numbers. Recognizing these scams protects your finances and identity.

Why It Matters:

- Prevents financial loss and unauthorized access to your accounts.
- Keeps your personal and financial information secure.

Tips:

1. Be cautious of unsolicited emails asking for sensitive information.
2. Verify the sender's email address and avoid clicking suspicious links.
3. Use multi-factor authentication for added account security.

Mindset Shift:
Suspicion isn't paranoia—it's protection against evolving threats.

"Phishing scams prey on trust—stay vigilant to keep your finances secure."

99. The Importance of Cybersecurity for Finances

Cybersecurity measures protect your financial accounts from hackers and online fraud. As digital transactions increase, so does the need for robust security.

Why It Matters:

- Prevents unauthorized access to your bank accounts, investments, or credit cards.
- Reduces the risk of financial losses from cyberattacks.

Tips:

1. Use strong, unique passwords for each financial account.
2. Enable two-factor authentication for added protection.
3. Avoid using public Wi-Fi for online banking or shopping.

Mindset Shift:
Cybersecurity isn't optional—it's a fundamental part of financial safety in a digital world.

"Strong cybersecurity practices protect more than money—they safeguard your peace of mind."

100. How to Create Strong Passwords for Online Accounts

A strong password combines upper and lowercase letters, numbers, and special characters. Avoid using easily guessable information like names or birthdays.

Why It Matters:

- Strong passwords prevent unauthorized access to your accounts.
- They reduce the likelihood of data breaches and financial theft.

Tips:

1. Use a password manager to create and store complex passwords securely.
2. Update passwords regularly to stay ahead of potential breaches.
3. Avoid reusing passwords across multiple accounts.

Mindset Shift:

Your password is your first line of defense—make it strong enough to withstand any attack.

"A strong password is your digital fortress—build it wisely to protect your financial world."

Chapter 11- Long-Term Planning

Long-Term Planning: Building a Strong Financial Future

For young individuals, it might feel like you have all the time in the world to figure out money and long-term planning. But the truth is, the habits and decisions you make now lay the foundation for your financial future. Developing a positive money mindset and learning how to plan long-term will help you achieve financial independence, reduce stress, and create opportunities you never thought possible. While thinking about the future might seem overwhelming, breaking it into manageable steps makes it easier—and starting early gives you an incredible advantage.

Why Start Long-Term Planning Now?

The earlier you start thinking about your finances, the more time you have to benefit from tools like *compound interest* and long-term investments. A small amount of money saved or invested today can grow exponentially over the years. For example, if you start investing $50 a month at 18 and earn an average annual return of 7%, you could have over $120,000 by age 50. If you wait until you're 30 to start, you'd have less than half that amount. Long-term planning isn't just about saving money—it's about building the skills, habits, and mindset that will guide your financial decisions for decades.

Steps to Build a Long-Term Money Mindset

Use the acronym **P.L.A.N.** to structure your approach to long-term financial planning:

- **P:** *Picture Your Future* – Start by imagining where you want to be in 5, 10, or 20 years. Do you want to own a home? Travel? Start a business? Having a vision helps you set clear goals.
- **L:** *Learn and Build Habits* – Financial literacy is key. Learn how budgeting, saving, and investing work. Build habits like saving a portion of every paycheck or tracking expenses.
- **A:** *Act with Intention* – Every financial decision you make should align with your goals. Avoid impulse spending and focus on purchases or investments that support your long-term vision.
- **N:** *Navigate Challenges* – Life will throw curveballs, but having a plan helps you stay on track. Build an emergency fund and stay flexible as your goals evolve.

Key Financial Strategies for Long-Term Success

1. **Start Saving Early**
   Even if you're only earning a little, get into the habit of saving. Open a savings account or high-yield savings account to grow your money. Aim to save at least 10-20% of what you earn. If you don't have a paycheck, save a portion of any gift money or allowances.

2. **Build an Emergency Fund**
   Life is unpredictable, and an emergency fund is your financial safety net. Aim to save $500-$1,000 as a starter fund, then work toward saving three to six months' worth of living expenses. Keep this money in a separate account so it's not accidentally spent.

3. **Learn About Investing**
   Investing might sound complicated, but starting young gives your money more time to grow. Platforms like Acorns, Robinhood, or Fidelity let you begin investing with small amounts. Focus on simple, diversified options like index funds or ETFs (Exchange-Traded Funds). Investing just $20-$50 a month can lead to significant growth over time.

4. **Set Clear Goals**
   Whether it's saving for a car, traveling, or starting your own business, set short-term, mid-term, and long-term financial goals. Write them down and break them into smaller, actionable steps. For example, if you want to save $5,000 for a car in three years, set a goal of saving $140 a month.

5. **Avoid Debt Traps**
   Credit cards and loans can be helpful, but they're also easy to misuse. If you get a credit card, only spend what you can pay off in full each month. High-interest debt can spiral out of control and set back your long-term plans.
6. **Develop Multiple Income Streams**
   Relying on one source of income can be risky. Consider creating multiple streams of income through side hustles, freelance work, or part-time jobs. Even small additional earnings can make a big difference when saved or invested.
7. **Build Financial Literacy**
   The more you know about money, the better decisions you'll make. Read books like *Rich Dad Poor Dad* by Robert Kiyosaki or *The Simple Path to Wealth* by JL Collins. Follow reputable financial influencers, take free online courses, or use apps like Mint to track your spending and budgeting.

Mindset Shifts for Long-Term Success

Developing a positive money mindset is just as important as financial strategies. Focus on seeing money as a tool to create opportunities rather than as a source of stress. Understand that small sacrifices today—like skipping an unnecessary purchase—can lead to significant rewards later.

Embrace a growth mindset, knowing that financial skills can always be learned and improved.

Practical Habits to Start Now

- Save a portion of every dollar you earn, no matter how small.
- Track your spending to understand where your money goes.
- Automate savings or investing to ensure consistency.
- Review your financial goals every six months to stay focused.
- Celebrate small wins, like hitting a savings milestone or paying off a bill, to stay motivated.

Final Thoughts

Long-term financial planning might not seem urgent when you're just starting out, but the earlier you begin, the more opportunities you create for yourself. By using the P.L.A.N. framework, saving consistently, avoiding unnecessary debt, and investing in your future, you're setting the stage for a life of financial independence and success. Remember, small steps now lead to big rewards later. Start building your habits and mindset today, and your future self will thank you.

Why Is Financial Education a Lifelong Journey?

Financial education is not a one-time lesson; it's a lifelong skill that evolves as you grow and as the world changes. For students, understanding money early lays the foundation for future success. As your responsibilities shift—from saving allowance to managing a paycheck or investing—staying informed helps you make better decisions, avoid mistakes, and seize opportunities.

101. Benefits of Lifelong Learning

1. **Adaptability**: Stay ready for new financial tools, like digital wallets or investing apps.
2. **Wealth Building**: Early knowledge of saving and investing grows your money over time.
3. **Mistake Prevention**: Avoid traps like high-interest debt or scams.

Tips for Staying Informed

- Read one financial book a year (*Rich Dad Poor Dad* is a great start).
- Follow podcasts like *How to Money* for quick tips.
- Use apps like Mint or Acorns to apply what you learn.

Steps to Start

1. Choose a topic: budgeting, saving, or investing.
2. Dedicate 10 minutes daily to learning.
3. Apply new knowledge to real-life decisions, like tracking expenses or opening a savings account.

Committing to financial education ensures you're ready for life's financial challenges and opportunities. Start small, stay curious, and watch your knowledge grow alongside your wealth.

"The earlier you learn about money, the more power you have to shape your financial future.

Start now to build the life you want!"

www.ingramcontent.com/pod-product-compliance
Lightning Source LLC
Chambersburg PA
CBHW071550220526
45469CB00003B/969